Of Minor Canons and Lay Clerks

The Singing Men of
Norwich Cathedral
Part I
1620 - 1819

Tom Roast

ISBN 978-0-9572781-0-3

Published by
Gateway Music Norwich

Contents

		Page
Preface		3
The Choir	The 1620 Statutes	4
	Towards the Interregnum	6
	The Choir Restored	8
	Humphrey Prideaux, Prebendary and Dean	10
	The Early Georgian Period	14
	The Beckwith Years	16
The Choirmen: other occupations and remuneration		20
The Minor Canons		24
The Lay Clerks		50
Bibliography		72

Of the Number of those persons who are maintained in the Cathedral Church of the Holy and Undivided Trinity of Norwich

First, We appoint and ordain that there be perpetually in Our said Cathedral Church one Dean, six Prebendaries, six Minor Canons, one Gospeller (Reader of the Gospel), one Epistoler, eight Lay Clerks, one Organist, eight Choristers, six Poor Men (to be nourished at the expense of the said Church), two Vergers, two Under-sacristans, one Doorkeeper, one Head Steward (a nobleman), one Under-steward of the Courts, one Clerk of the Chapter: two Cooks, one Butler, one Caterer, one Baliff of the Liberties, one Auditor and Ingrosser of the Accounts, who is also to be Surveyor of the Lands and Woods, one Keeper of the Ferry, one Beadle of the Poor Men, who shall also work the bellows of the organ. These persons shall diligently serve in the same Church in the appointed number, each in his order, according to Our statutes and ordinances; and before their admission they shall severally take the oath.

Statutes of Norwich Cathedral 1620, Chapter I

Preface

The period covered by this study begins in 1620 when a new set of statutes ordering the cathedral's governance was granted to Norwich Cathedral by King James I. It ends in 1819, the year which saw the death of the last serving member of the influential Beckwith family. Much of the information on this period has been drawn from three unpublished sources: firstly, the Dean and Chapter Archive held at Norfolk Record Office and in particular the Chapter Books (DCN 24/2-24/6) and the Audit Books (DCN 11/1-11/16) which record the appointment and conduct of the choirmen and the payment of their salaries; secondly, a dissertation by Andrew Cornall for a degree at the University of East Anglia entitled *The Practice of Music at Norwich Cathedral c. 1558-1649*, which throws much light on the period between the Dissolution and the Civil War, and gives the names of the choirmen prior to the Interregnum; thirdly, the notebooks kept by Dr A H Mann on Norwich Cathedral musicians which are also held at Norfolk Record Office (Mann Mss. 430-432).

Where necessary pre-1752 dates have been amended to conform to the present calendar.

The following abbreviations have been used:

AC	Alumni Cantabrigiensis (see Bibliography)
AO	Alumni Oxoniensis (see Bibliography)
BL	British Library
CSPD	Calendar of State Papers, Domestic
DCN	The Dean and Chapter Archive at Norfolk Record Office
G.Mag	The Gentleman's Magazine
GRO	General Register Office
NC	The Norfolk Chronicle
NG	The Norwich Gazette
NM	Norwich Mercury
NRO	Norfolk Record Office
ODNB	Oxford Dictionary of National Biography
W & C-H	Williams and Cozens-Hardy (see Bibliography)

The Choir

The 1620 Statutes

It took nearly a century for Norwich Cathedral to acquire an authoritative set of statutes. When the Benedictine priory was dissolved in 1538 the entire establishment was taken over as a cathedral of the New Foundation with the prior and monks becoming the dean and chapter. A set of statutes was drawn up during the reign of Henry VIII and this set down the number of persons required to sing in the choir. Under Queen Elizabeth a new code was drafted but apparently never officially sanctioned. A further set, based on both Henrician and Elizabethan models and probably reflecting existing practice, was drafted by Dean Suckling and granted by James I in 1620, though it took a few more years and a number of minor amendments before the details were finally confirmed.[1] The musical establishment was now formalized at six minor canons (priests or deacons), one gospeller, one epistoler, eight lay clerks, eight choirboys and an organist, an arrangement which pertained (other than the occasional employment of supernumerary singers) until the number of minor canons was reduced in the mid nineteenth century.[2] This level of staffing was not dissimilar to the choirs of other provincial cathedrals at this time: at Salisbury there were six priests, seven laymen and eight choristers; at Wells the numbers were 6: 8: 6 and at Lichfield 6: 10: 8.[3] The statutes specified that the sixteen adult singers should include five basses, five tenors and five countertenors; the extra voice was to be a bass or countertenor as no more than five tenors were permitted. It was expected that the men would be educated, of good reputation, and skilled in the art of singing. Each person was required to be permanently resident and provided with a house in the precincts. Minor canons were allowed to hold one outside benefice. The gospeller, whose duties naturally involved reading the gospel, had to be in holy orders and normally held a junior position on the clergy side of the choir with the expectation of a full minor canon's place when one became available. The epistoler was usually the most senior lay clerk, though the post was occupied at various times by both ordained and lay singers. Finally, one man from the choir was appointed master of the choristers and

---

1. See Houlbrooke, pp. 530-533
2. A printed copy of the statutes in Latin and English is at Norfolk Record Office (NRO), DCN 28/1.
3. Le Huray, pp. 14-15

he was responsible for the boys' welfare, education and musical training.

The statutes were received at the cathedral with great pomp on 5 September 1620. The bishop, the dean, the prebendaries and all other officers of the cathedral assembled in the chapter house for the reading of the statutes by Robert Smyth, the chapter clerk. All attending were then required to take a prescribed oath, including the members of the choir who stood as follows: six minor canons - William Fugill, Richard Bracket, Thomas Sadlington, George Saunders, William Merrick and John Woodson; gospeller John Sowter; epistoler John Carlton; and seven lay clerks - Thomas Moody, Peter Sandley, Thomas Purton, John Carlton, Martin Carlton, Redmaine Carlton and John Haund. The organists were William Cobbold and William Inglott.[4] One lay clerk was missing from the ceremony: Thomas Quash took his oath a month later.

The daily routine of services was a reading of morning prayer at 6am (later in winter) and sung services of matins at 9am and evening prayer at 4pm. On Sundays and feast days the service was more elaborate, and on Christmas Day the cathedral had the assistance of the City Waits. Celebration of the eucharist was rarely observed.[5] Under the statutes all members of the choir were expected to attend on Sundays and feast days but on weekdays one countertenor, one tenor and one bass could be absent in turn for a whole week without penalty, and three minor canons could be absent daily in turn to attend to their parish duties. The stipends they received were £10 for a minor canon, £9 for the gospeller, £8 10s. for the epistoler and £8 for a lay clerk. Fines for unauthorised absence were to be deducted at the rate of 2d. on weekdays, 4d. on Sundays, and 6d. on double feast days (identified as Christmas Day, Easter Day, Ascension Day and others) though it is not clear if these were enforced. There were further fines for arriving late, leaving early, and not attending the sermon. Admonitions were given by the dean for misconduct and any person receiving three reprimands would normally be expelled from the choir. Discipline was sometimes a problem in the 1620s with two minor canons being particularly troublesome to the dean - William Fugill for neglect of his duty and drunkenness, and Thomas Sadlington for rudeness and adultery. Richard Gibbs, who was appointed organist in 1622, was admonished for allowing lay clerk Peter Sandley to play in his absence, Sandley being the worse for drink and causing confusion during the service.[6]

---

4. Williams and Cozens-Hardy, p. 54
5. Atherton and Morgan, pp. 544-545
6. Williams and Cozens-Hardy, passim

Towards the Interregnum

The order and ceremony at the cathedral established it as a bastion of religious orthodoxy, bolstered by the performing of elaborate music in an opulent setting. This placed it at odds with the civic authorities and radical Protestant groups within the city who had set up a parallel form of ministry by providing their own preachers and lecturers as a response to what they saw as a return to Romish practices by a church not yet fully reformed. Relations worsened when Bishop Harsnett sought to put down alternative preachers by ordering that all Sunday services in city churches should end by 9.30am so that everyone could attend the sermon at the cathedral. In 1637 Charles I ordered the corporation to attend the entire cathedral service each Sunday, not just the sermon, and to endure the winter cold and the extreme length of the service. Extra room in the choir was provided by the building of two-tier galleries across the ends of the transepts, but such was the heightened tension towards some in the corporation that the mayor and aldermen and their wives, seated in the lower tier, were subjected to various objects being dropped or thrown from the upper galleries. The attempt at forcing conformity upon the people of Norwich caused overcrowding and led to a state of disorder which was the very opposite of the orthodoxy for which the church stood. In addition to their religious differences, the cathedral and the corporation were involved in long-running disputes concerning the boundaries of their respective jurisdictions.[7] But these local issues were to be overtaken by events at a national level. From the time of the Long Parliament in 1640 the whole church hierarchy came under attack in the punitive 'root and branch' reforms. In 1643 parliamentary troops, aided by local supporters including some of the corporation, ransacked the cathedral, breaking down the organ and burning the choirbooks. The events were graphically described four years later by Bishop Joseph Hall.

> It is no other than tragical to relate the carriage of that furious sacrilege, whereof our eyes and ears were the sad witnesses, under the authority and presence of Linsey, Toftes the sheriff, and Greenwood. Lord what work was here, what clattering of glasses, what beating down of walls, what tearing up of monuments, what pulling down of seats, what wresting out of irons and brass from the windows and graves,... what toting and piping upon the destroyed organ pipes, and what a hideous triumph on the market day before all the country, when in a

---

7.   Atherton and Morgan, pp. 541-557

kind of sacrilegious and profane procession, all the organ pipes, vestments, both copes and surplices,... and the service books and singing books that could be had, were carried to the fire in the public market place; a lewd wretch walking before the train, in his cope, trailing in the dirt, with a service book in his hand, imitating, in an impious scorn, the tune, and usurping the words of the Litany, used formerly in the church.[8]

The bishop was ejected from his palace and he retreated to what is now the Dolphin Inn at Heigham. By 1649 the positions of dean and prebendaries, and all minor cathedral officials, had been abolished.

The effect on the members of the choir was calamitous. Left with few or no duties after the destruction of the organ, some went off to look for employment elsewhere. In 1644 the dean and chapter paid the salaries of Joseph Reding and William Alsey to their families as both men had been absent for several months.[9] In 1646 Reding was deprived of his benefice of St Augustine's for taking sides with the royalist forces.[10] The last available account for the period shows that all sixteen adult members of the choir, and organist Richard Gibbs, were still receiving their full salaries for the year to Michaelmas 1646.[11] A Parliamentary Survey of dean and chapter properties carried out in 1649 recorded the names of the organist, three minor canons and eight lay clerks as being householders within the precincts, although only three of them - George Saunders, Martin Carlton and Lawrence Harman - were actually in residence.[12] The impecunious state of the musicians became so acute that in 1657 the Trustees for the Maintenance of Ministers awarded the sum of £20 to be shared between two minor canons and seven lay clerks.[13]

---

8. *Bishop Hall's Hard Measure* (1647) in Joseph Hall, *Satires*, London (1824), p. 87.
9. Williams and Cozens-Hardy, p.84
10 Matthews, p.272
11. NRO, DCN 10/2/1
12. Metters, pp. 31-34
13. Matthews, p. 12. Two minor canons - Smyth and Horne - received £4 and £2 respectively.
    Lay clerks Sandley, Beck and R and M Carlton received £2 10s., Alsey and Meares £1 10s., and Mowting £1.

The Choir Restored

The proclamation of King Charles II on 8 May 1660 was received in Norwich with much rejoicing. The new dean and prebendaries were appointed by mid July and the chapter held its first meeting on 7 August. One of their first tasks was to re-establish choral services in the cathedral and in this respect they were fortunate that six of the lay clerks from the 1643 choir - Peter Sandley, Anthony Beck, William Alsey, Redmaine and Martin Carlton and Thomas Mowting - were still living. In December 1660 they appointed Samuel Norman and Samuel Newman, thereby quickly bringing the lay clerks back to full strength. Choristers also made an early reappearance: Peter Sandley was awarded £4 in November 1661 for teaching them for the past year. However, the re-forming of the clergy side of the choir took much longer. For a start only two minor canons - Thomas Horne and Edward Smyth - were available. Furthermore, new appointments were probably delayed until livings in the grant of the dean and chapter, from which the minor canons augmented their incomes, became available. Two clergymen, Christopher Stinnet and Robert Snelling, were appointed in 1661. In the same year, in an apparent attempt to boost numbers, the dean admitted two additional lay clerks, but their positions were never confirmed as this would have been in breach of the statutes.[14] Norwich was not alone in struggling to secure the services of minor canons. At Winchester there were only four canons in 1662 instead of six 'because two pettycanons (who are required to be in full orders, yet well instructed in music) cannot as yet be found.'[15] In 1662 the chapter came up with its own answer to the problem: it ordained three of its lay clerks as deacons - William Alsey, Samuel Newman and Anthony Beck - and appointed them as minor canons. Three further lay clerks were soon admitted in their places. However, by this time Horne and Smyth were no longer in the choir (probably deceased) and with the departure of Snelling in 1664 the minor canons were still only four in number. More appointments were made in the ensuing years with mixed success; three men stayed for less than a year and one, Thomas Housden, was dismissed for frequent drunkenness and for deserting the choir. Numbers remained at four or five until 1673 when, with the appointment of Gawen Nash, the singing clergymen were numerically complete.

---

14. NRO,DCN 24/3, f. 29v shows a Thomas Morley and Thomas More admitted by the dean but no payments were recorded in the Audit Books.
15. Ian Spink, *Restoration Cathedral Music 1660-1714*, Oxford (1995), p. 361

Even with six minor canons and eight lay clerks the choir still lacked the singers who officiated as gospeller and epistoler. For many years two of the minor canons were paid an additional allowance to fulfil these functions. However, with the accession of William and Mary to the throne in 1688 a conflict arose between the cathedral's statutes, under which the gospeller was to be a deacon and the epistoler a layman, and a new Act of Uniformity which ordered that a priest should read both the gospel and the epistle. As a result the places were left unfilled and the salaries which would have been paid were appropriated for repairs to the fabric of the cathedral. The matter dragged on into the next century and it was only after the King's death that the dean declared in June 1704 that he intended to fill the vacant places. The epistoler's place was quickly awarded to Richard Sparrow, but the dean wanted Benjamin Noble to be gospeller. Noble was in Maryland at the time and it was expected that he would return to Norwich the following Spring. When he failed to do so the dean appointed Thomas Dunch, but Dunch was immediately given leave of absence to continue his studies at Cambridge and it was another ten years before he took up his duties at Norwich. Finally, in February 1712, the dean appointed Henry Fish as gospeller. Only then did the choir possess, for the first time since 1643, its full complement of singers as required by the statutes.

A key part of the task of re-establishing choral services in the 1660s concerned the appointment of an organist. For this important post the dean and chapter looked outside and secured the services of the experienced Richard Ayleward who was formally admitted as organist and master of the choristers in March 1661, though he may have commenced his duties before the end of 1660.[16] Ayleward was born in 1626, the son of a minor canon at Winchester Cathedral, and from 1638 until the outbreak of the Civil War he was a cathedral chorister at Winchester under Christopher Gibbons. It is not known where he went during the Interregnum but it is probable that he enjoyed some form of private patronage. Upon his appointment at Norwich he was assigned a house in the precincts, and considerable sums were spent by the chapter on putting the house into good repair. For a reason which is not clear, he gave up his positions in 1664. The Audit Books for the year show that a small sum was paid by the chapter 'in sending for Mr. Ayleward at the assizes'. Whatever the reason for his absence, Ayleward was reappointed to his former positions when Thomas Gibbs, who had succeeded

---

16. The Audit Books show that Ayleward was paid for a full year ending Michaelmas 1661.

him, died of the plague in 1666. Ayleward himself died in 1669 and was buried in the cathedral. He was a significant composer, producing twenty verse anthems, three service settings and some keyboard music. The majority of the anthems make considerable demands on resources and it must be doubtful whether they were within the capability of the cathedral choir which was still being rebuilt: they were probably written during the Interregnum. On the other hand, some of the liturgical music was performed at Norwich, and Ayleward's setting of the Preces and Responses has found an established place in the repertory of most present-day cathedral choirs.[17]

The other vital element at this time was the replacement of the organ which had been torn down in 1643, and again the dean and chapter acted decisively by purchasing a temporary instrument from Richard Plum of Bury St Edmunds in 1661 at a cost of £70.[18] This was replaced in 1664 by a new instrument built by Dallam which was erected on the screen where the old organ had stood. Music books made an early reappearance: in the account to Michaelmas 1662 payment was made for six service books for the choir. In 1664 further payments were made for binding the choirbooks, and an inventory taken in 1666 listed a total of 54 books of services and anthems in the care of the precentor, William Rampley.[19] Thus, by the mid 1660s Norwich Cathedral had a new organ, an accomplished organist, a choir of twelve men and (probably) eight choristers, and a substantial collection of music books. It represented a notable success for the dean and chapter.

Humphrey Prideaux, Prebendary and Dean

In the forty years covering the end of the seventeenth century and the beginning of the eighteenth century, the choir - along with most other aspects of cathedral life - came under the influence of Humphrey Prideaux, prebendary from 1681 and dean from 1702 until his death in 1724. Prideaux was a man of strong conviction and he administered the cathedral's affairs in a robust manner. He was, moreover, a disciplinarian who believed that his predecessors had been lax in punishing abuses and misconduct. As a result, the chapter records for this period are littered with reprimands, admonitions, and expulsions handed down to minor cathedral officials.

---

17. See Roast 1, chapter IV.
18. See *The Musical Times*, 1 November 1904, p. 704.
19. Oxford, Bodleian Library, Tanner Ms. 133, f. 187v

Absenteeism from the choir was a problem for the chapter and from Michaelmas 1685 they invoked the statutes and punished non-attenders with a pecuniary fine. The precentor, John Parris, as a result of his diligent attendance, was entrusted with taking a note of all absences and for this he was allowed to pocket the fines. A lack of respect for authority was also an issue. It had become customary during the 1680s to collect alms at the doors of the cathedral on certain days for the poor of the city, and four lay clerks were appointed by the dean to stand at the doors to receive the offerings. But on Easter Sunday 1688, following the bishop's exhortation in his sermon for the congregation to be generous in their giving, the lay clerks, in an act of open disobedience, refused to take their places at the doors. The four men - Charles Alden, Richard Blagrave, Francis Knights and James Wyth - were called before the dean and chapter and severely admonished. Knights was given a second admonition for threatening to beat up the verger who had delivered the dean's instructions.[20] A more far-reaching problem for the choir arose in 1688 when James II was replaced on the throne by William and Mary. A bill passed through parliament the following year required all clergy to swear an oath of allegiance to the new monarchs. Many refused, including minor canons Gawen Nash and John Shaw, on the grounds that they had made an oath to King James which they believed must hold as long as he lived. Both men were expelled from the choir and deprived of their livings.[21] A third minor canon, John Connould, was twice admonished for not reading the prayer for the King, and when, during assize week, he refused to do so in front of the judge and justices of the peace, he too was expelled though he was allowed to retain his parishes.

With Humphrey Prideaux's elevation to dean in 1702 the punishments meted out to errant choirmen were stepped up, beginning with the unpleasant case of minor canon John Stukeley who had been exposing himself to the women of the precincts. After taking evidence from a number of witnesses and holding several hearings, Prideaux expelled Stukeley from the cathedral. Another minor canon, Peter Burgess, was admonished for getting Stukeley to baptize his child, knowing that he had been expelled. Prideaux also had to deal with the case of lay clerk Richard Blagrave who had lost his voice, 'being spoiled by the pox for which he ought to have been expelled by the last dean'. Prideaux felt unable to dismiss Blagrave and allowed him to retain his place in the choir by using a deputy.

20. This was the most serious act of defiance by the lay clerks since 1608 when they had threatened to go on strike. See Williams and Cozens-Hardy, p. 43.
21. Overton, pp. 487 and 492

The next problem concerned lay clerk William Pleasants who was also master of the choristers. Pleasants was reported to be making inappropriate statements, asserting that 'the clergy did preach up hell only to fright the people'. He was also accused of groping the codpiece of one of the choristers. Again Prideaux collected evidence and summoned Pleasants to the chapter house where he was made to kneel in front of the choir and make a full confession. He was dismissed as master of the choristers but kept his place in the choir. Another offender was minor canon John Blagrave who had replaced John Stukeley. Blagrave had become 'a common haunter of alehouses, taverns, and other houses of debauchery and disorder', causing many people to stay away from the cathedral when he was reading the service or administering the sacraments. The dean gave him two admonitions and then, in March 1712, when his behaviour resulted in his arrest and imprisonment, Prideaux expelled him from the church. Two minor canons resigned in 1715 rather than face expulsion - Francis Folchier for fathering a child with his maidservant, and Charles Tillet for his inappropriate relationship with the wife of a Norwich waggoner. One appointment made by Prideaux seems to have contravened the statutes which required all new members of the choir to be skilled in singing. When Philip Burroughs was admitted as a minor canon in 1715 he promised 'that I will, under a skilful master, learn to sing'. According to his colleague John Fox 'he made a show of learning to sing for a while, but never sang either anthem or service'.[22] His time in the choir was ended by an accident in 1718 when he was thrown from his horse and died from a broken skull.[23]

In 1703, as a means of injecting greater order into the cathedral's music, Prideaux instructed the precentor to prepare a weekly list of anthems and services, together with the names of the singers expected to be present, and on receiving the dean's approval to post it prominently in the vestry. In 1714 he summoned the choir and laid down the demeanor required from them during worship. In particular they were ordered to stand at the singing of hymns, psalms and anthems; to kneel reverently during prayers; to have their surplices washed regularly; and to attend at the chapter house after service on Saturday evenings. This was Prideaux's last recorded remonstrance with the choirmen other than an admonition given to Philip Priest in 1721 for poor attendance. In his first twelve years he had handed out more punishments than any other dean, but his last ten

22. NRO, DCN 33/5
23. NRO, DCN 115/3, p. 61

years showed him as a man in decline caused by age and ill health. Yet his determination to enforce a stricter rule of conduct within the cathedral community was not without compassion and understanding. Having expelled John Stukeley, Prideaux allowed him to remain in his house in the precincts; and Richard Blagrave should have been dismissed but Prideaux feared that he might starve if he lost his job. 'Men will always be sinners' he mused, 'and as long as clergymen are men, they will be so too'.[24]

Choir numbers during this period were maintained in accordance with the statutes except for two brief periods when an extra voice was added. John Wilson, who had been a chorister under Richard Ayleward in the late 1660s, was granted a special place in the choir in 1675 as a probationer until a lay clerk's place became vacant. He sang in this capacity for four years but no vacancy occurred and he left in 1679. He was succeeded by James Cooper for whom a place fell vacant the following year. In 1722 Edward Payne was engaged as a supernumerary lay clerk to attend the choir once a day, a position he occupied for three years. These were one-off appointments and it was not until much later in the eighteenth century that supernumerary singers became a regular part of the choir.

An indication of the music being sung at the cathedral in Prideaux's time comes from two principal sources. Firstly, there exists a set of eight partbooks and an organ book formerly belonging to Norwich Cathedral which came into the hands of Dr A H Mann and are now kept at King's College, Cambridge.[25] The books begin with the anthems and services composed by Richard Ayleward which, as seen above, were probably written during the Interregnum. Thereafter the pieces were copied into the books between around 1670 and 1720. As would be expected, national figures such as William Byrd, Thomas Morley, Orlando Gibbons and John Blow are there, but a remarkably high proportion of the pieces are by Norwich musicians, and of these the verse anthems of lay clerk John Jackson, minor canon John Connould, and lay clerk turned organist James Cooper are especially revealing. The principal characteristic of the verse anthem is the division of the text between verses for solo voices and choruses for full choir, all supported by an organ accompaniment. Jackson's anthems from the 1670s, like those of Ayleward, show inventive solo parts with choruses that usually involve some interesting

24. Atherton and Morgan, p. 573
25. Cambridge, King's College, Rowe Library Mss. 9-17. See P. Oboussier, *The Rowe and Mann Music Library, King's College, Cambridge: A Catalogue of Musical Manuscripts* (typescript), Cambridge and London (1952-53).

part-movement. With the anthems of Connould, which come from a slightly later period, the verses retain their expressive character but the length and complexity of the choruses is much reduced. This trend is taken a stage further by Cooper who composed not less than 26 anthems. His short choruses of simple harmony merely repeat the last phrase of the text from the preceding verse. It is not difficult to see a link here between a choir that had become slack in its conduct and a style of anthem which could be performed with a minimum of preparation. Composers of greater ability would have created works of some stature in spite of these constraints; unfortunately, the simpler textures serve to highlight the weaknesses of Connould and Cooper by exposing their poor word-setting and occasional ungainly part-writing.[26] The second useful source of information is a handwritten book of anthem texts compiled by Richard Blagrave which he called *Cantica Sacra or Divine Anthems usually sung in the Cathedral Church of Norwich, 1690*.[27] It contains the words of 39 anthems (but no music) and most texts have a composer's name appended. It probably represents a snapshot view of the repertory in this particular year. A few major composers are included, with two anthems by Henry Purcell, one by Gibbons, and six by the increasingly popular Michael Wise. Of the lesser figures, fourteen pieces are by local musicians - one by Ayleward, four by Jackson, six by Cooper and three by Blagrave himself.

The early success of the re-formed choir of the 1660s had, by the beginning of the eighteenth century, given way to an unsettled period characterized by poor attendance, a lack of discipline, and some obviously unsuitable appointments. It was a time also when the choir's repertory had become watered down by the inclusion of some amateurish works written by local musicians. By 1720, in spite of Dean Prideaux's exertions, music at the cathedral had reached a low point.

The Early Georgian Period

The half-century between 1720 and 1770 seems to have been a relatively uneventful time in the cathedral's musical history. With the decline and death of Humphrey Prideaux the number of disciplinary actions dropped sharply, and chapter business regarding the choirmen was mainly concerned with appointments, the allocation of houses in the precincts, and the presentation of

---

26. For more on these local composers see Roast 1.
27. Oxford, Bodleian Library, Tanner Ms. 401

minor canons to local benefices. Some disciplinary measures were, however, still necessary. Gilbert Pickering, a former precentor, received admonitions for absenteeism, for not wearing his proper degree hood over his surplice,[28] and for rude behaviour: he resigned in 1727. Minor reprimands were given to John Pleasants for rudeness and to Richard Deere for poor attendance. Two minor canons were expelled - John Brooke in 1747 for desertion, and Cropley Hatch in 1755 for leaving his residence in the precincts and moving into the Gatehouse public house. The dean and prebendaries now approached matters of administration in a more measured and subdued way. Most of the deans had reached the extent of their abilities and ambition, while many of the prebendaries (who were required to be in residence at Norwich for just two months a year) held their stalls for long periods, some of them achieving remarkable longevity.[29] Throughout these years choir numbers were maintained at the statutory level, and the basic salaries paid to the choirmen were unchanged from those set before the Interregnum. The two organists - Humphrey Cotton and Thomas Garland - divided their time between the cathedral and secular music making in the city. Both were involved in the growing number of music societies and both performed at benefit and subscription concerts.[30] For fifty years musical life at the cathedral made no real advances other than the enlargement of the choir's repertoire through the acquisition of some printed collections of music, and the copying of new vocal parts into the choirbooks.

The dean and chapter accounts contain many payments relating to the purchase of music books. Some books may simply have had ruled pages for completion by copyists, and some entries are vague or ambiguous, but the purchase of several printed collections can be identified. The earliest acquisition was in 1680 when payment was made 'for carriage of Thomkins set of music books bringing from London'. This would have referred to the collection *Musica Deo Sacra* by Thomas Tomkins which was published posthumously in 1668. A full set of ten books survives at the cathedral, though they show few signs of having been used to any great extent. In 1726 the cathedral acquired William Croft's *Musica Sacra*, followed by Maurice Greene's *Forty Select Anthems* in 1743. The purchase of 'Handel's Te Deum in Score' in 1769 probably refers to the Dettingen Te Deum which was very popular in Norwich in the later decades of the eighteenth century.

---

28. Under part 16 of the statutes graduates were required to wear the hood appropriate to their degree.
29. Wilson, pp. 583-587
30. See Fawcett, passim.

The most important and influential published collections at this time were the three volumes of *Cathedral Music* compiled by William Boyce which appeared in 1760, 1768 and 1773. Norwich was one of a small number of cathedrals that failed to subscribe to their original publication.[31] The volumes would, however, have been available at the cathedral as Thomas Garland, the organist, was a subscriber. The dean and chapter certainly acquired the books, probably in 1789, and subsequently added several copies of the second edition.

The earliest manuscript music in the cathedral library is an assortment of sixteen partbooks which were compiled between about 1720 and 1790.[32] Unfortunately, no complete set of books survives, and some volumes are only loosely related in their contents. It was the job of one of the lay clerks to copy music into the books, and the names of most of the copyists can be identified from payments recorded in the cathedral's accounts. The books show the popularity of Croft, Blow and Wise as well as John Weldon, William Child and Henry Aldrich. Norwich composers are represented by William Inglott, Ayleward, Jackson, Connould, Cooper, Pleasants and Cotton. There are also pieces by the Ely composers James Hawkins and Thomas Bullis.

The Beckwith Years

A number of developments took place during the 1770s to suggest that music was beginning to occupy a more important place in cathedral life. From 1771 the choir was strengthened by the regular employment of a supernumerary lay clerk. An extra singing boy was added in 1785 and by 1788 there were two additional choristers. In 1772 the governors of the newly-opened Norfolk and Norwich Hospital instituted an annual sermon to be preached in the cathedral at which a collection was taken for hospital funds. The following year music was added to the sermon and within a few years it became an annual large-scale performance of sacred music which ran until 1823.[33] By 1770 the Beckwith family had come to the forefront of music in the cathedral. At least twelve members of the family were practising musicians; for twenty years from 1762 there were four Beckwiths in the choir; and for a century from 1719 the cathedral was never without a Beckwith on

---

31. This is confirmed by the list of subscribers. Bumpus, p. 262, believed that Bangor, Carlisle,
    St David's, Llandaff, Norwich and Wells were the only cathedrals that did not subscribe.
32. Music Mss. 1-16. See Roast 4.
33. For an account of the hospital charity services see Roast 3.

its musical staff.[34] Edward Beckwith was a lay clerk who became master of the choristers in 1759. His son, John 'Christmas' Beckwith,[35] was sent to Oxford where he received his musical training from William and Philip Hayes. In 1784 Edward was admonished for neglecting his duties, and the dean and chapter took the bold step of inviting his son to return to Norwich to take up a specially created post of assistant master of the choristers with particular responsibilities for the boys' musical training, leaving his father the job of giving them their general education. It was a masterstroke. John 'Christmas' Beckwith was a highly accomplished musician and he brought to Norwich his outstanding skills as a performer (on the organ and harpsichord), teacher, singer (he was a lay clerk), conductor and composer.

The decade of the 1770s also saw the appointment of a number of distinguished and scholarly minor canons. James Williams Newton published two collections of music as well as a guide to the Hebrew language; John Walker had a collection of his own poetry published in 1809; Henry Harington was a doctor of divinity; and Charles Millard had been a chorister at Magdalen College, Oxford and had sung a duet with the prima donna Signora Frasi. They were followed by Ozias Linley and Charles Smyth, both notable composers, and by Francis Howes whose publications included translations of works by Horace. A description of the choir, written by an unnamed author around 1795, shows a remarkably healthy state of affairs.

> Well do I remember, says an ear-witness, the delight with which I used to listen to the service in Norwich Cathedral, when the minor canons, eight in number, filed off into their stalls, precentor Millard at their head, whose admirable style and correct taste as a singer I have never heard surpassed; Browne's majestic tenor; Whittingham's sweet alto; and Hansell's sonorous bass; while Walker's silver tone and admirable recitation found their way into every corner of the huge building. Vaughan was then first boy, who acquired his musical knowledge and pure style under his master, Beckwith. Frequently, it would happen that the entire music of the day was written by members of the choir, for Garland, the organist (a pupil of Greene), was a composer of no mean talent. Beckwith, then master of the boys, was a most accomplished extempore player on the organ, and his well-known anthem 'The Lord is very great' sufficiently attests his talent as a writer for the church, and of the minor canons and lay clerks four had produced services.[36]

---

34. See Roast 2.
35. The name 'Christmas' was probably a sobriquet as a result of his birth on 25 December 1759.
36. *The English Cathedral Service, its Glory, its Decline and its Designed Extinction*, London (1845), p. 30. The reference to eight minor canons includes gospeller and epistoler.

During this time the choir occasionally went outside the cathedral to take part in local events. They attended at the opening of a new peal of bells at St Peter Mancroft in 1775; they joined with other choirs in the Grand Musical Festivals held in Norwich in 1788 and 1790; and a number of choristers performed at the opening of new organs by Beckwith at Halesworth in 1785 and Beccles in 1795.[37] Several members of the choir, mainly minor canons, belonged to The Harmonic Society, which flourished between 1784 and 1798, and its successor The Cathedral Club, which was active from 1815 to 1832. These groups met fortnightly during the winter months for supper, music making and intellectual discourse.[38]

The choir's repertoire continued to expand with the dean and chapter subscribing to collections of anthems by James Kent (1773), James Nares (1778), William Boyce (1780 and 1790), William Hayes (1795), John Clarke-Whitfield (1800 and 1805) and Thomas Ebdon (1810). The chapter also supported their own musicians by purchasing Beckwith's *Six Anthems* (c.1785) and *The First Verse of Every Psalm* (1808), and Charles Smyth's *Chants Single and Double* (1819). Many pieces from these collections were copied into the choirbooks.

In 1789 the cathedral published its first printed book of texts, intended specifically to enable the congregation to follow the words of the anthems being performed at divine service. Entitled *Anthems used in the Cathedral Church of Norwich*, the original printing contained 220 texts, each text being prefaced with the name of one or more composers. It seems that the compilers of the book drew heavily upon the published eighteenth-century collections which the cathedral had acquired, and it may not therefore be a completely true reflection of what was actually being sung. The composers most numerously featured are Greene (40 anthems), Croft (23), Nares (20), Boyce (15) and Kent (13). Local composers included are John 'Christmas' Beckwith (10 anthems), his uncle, lay clerk John Beckwith II (26), organist Thomas Garland (7) and minor canon James Williams Newton (2). From an earlier period there are pieces by James Cooper and William Pleasants. An appendix containing a further 170 texts was printed around 1817 and bound-in with the 1789 edition. Handel is now the prominent composer with seventeen texts (there were just two in the original book) plus Hugh Bond's twelve arrangements from Handel's oratorios. Other popular composers are Ebdon (16 pieces) and William Hayes (14). There are two more anthems by 'Christmas' Beckwith and one by John Beckwith II. No other local composers are featured.

---

37. *NM*, 24 June 1775, 4 June 1785, 26 July 1788, 17 July 1790 and 23 May 1795.
38. NRO, DCN 39/54

The wordbook underwent two further minor revisions and remained in use until it was replaced by an entirely new publication in 1859.

In October 1819, upon the death of organist John Charles Beckwith (the last member of the Beckwith family to serve the cathedral) and at the end of the period under consideration, the choir stood at full strength as follows. Six minor canons - Peter Hansell (precentor), Charles Smyth (sacrist), William Fitt Drake, Francis Howes, George Carter and George Day; gospeller Charles Freeman Millard; epistoler Paul Whittingham; and eight lay clerks - Richard Browne, Samuel Hayden, Samuel Blyth, William Sayer, Edward Woodward, John Cox, James Cupper and William Fenn.

Simple floor slab to Anthony Beck, lay clerk, minor canon, precentor and sacrist.

The Choirmen: other occupations and remuneration

Minor Canons

Under the provisions of the 1620 statutes, the minor canons were allowed to hold one ecclesiastical benefice situated not more than twelve miles from Norwich. From the start, abuse of this rule seems to have been tacitly accepted. With their cathedral salaries fixed at ten pounds a year throughout the entire period (nine pounds for the gospeller), the minor canons relied on outside parishes to make ends meet. Most of the livings granted were those under the patronage of the dean and chapter who held some thirty-eight benefices in Norfolk including thirteen within the city of Norwich.[39] The value of these livings varied widely: in 1780 the impoverished Norwich parish of St John Timberhill was worth £25 a year, while the combined benefice of Trowse with Lakenham produced an income of £136.[40] This inevitably led to jockeying for the better-endowed benefices,[41] and to the holding of several livings at the same time. This latter practice is well illustrated in the career of William Herne. Between the years 1728 and 1762 he accumulated the parishes of Horningtoft, Hemblington, Norwich St James and St Paul, Garveston and Alderford with Attlebridge. Both Horningtoft and Garveston lie more than twelve miles from Norwich. At the time of his last appointment he was 63 years old, and he retained all the livings, while still serving the cathedral as minor canon, precentor (briefly), sacrist and librarian, until his death at the age of 76.

In addition to their salary each minor canon received a dividend of ten pounds a year out of the corn rents received from the chapter's estates. They were provided with a house in the precincts or, if one was not available, given a cash allowance instead. Other positions within the cathedral were held by the minor canons, including those of precentor and sacrist, each post carrying a salary of one pound a year. The sacrist was also paid for washing the cathedral's linen. In the latter years of the seventeenth century a library was established for use by the dean and prebendaries: from 1710 a minor canon held the job of librarian, again at one pound a year (ten pounds from 1818). The person who read the daily office of morning prayer at 6 am was paid six pounds (eight pounds from 1679). Preaching brought occasional fees with the sum of one pound being paid to the clergyman

---

39. See Dawson Turner.
40. NRO, DCN 33/21, List of minor canons' preferments.
41. This is illustrated in a long statement from the Reverend John Fox in the 1720s. See NRO, DCN 33/5.

who delivered the Good Friday and Rogation Day sermons at the cathedral: between 1788 and 1811 the Good Friday sermon was always given by one of the minor canons. Several of the clergy, especially those newly arrived from university, were invited by Norwich Corporation to deliver Hall's Sacramental Lectures, a year's worth of monthly sermons preached alternately at four city churches.[42] For this they received ten pounds, a sum equal to their salary from the cathedral. Finally, they received small fees for attending at the installation of a bishop (two shillings) and archdeacon (one shilling and eight pence), plus a dinner on the day.

The hierarchical structure of the cathedral's governance, with its clear division between the minor canons and the dean and prebendaries, meant that the minor canons, many of whom were appointed straight from Oxford or Cambridge, received no preferment and usually died in office. In spite of acquiring the same degrees as the prebendaries, and being responsible for conducting the twice-daily services at the cathedral, not one of them seems to have stepped up to a prebendal stall at Norwich or anywhere else.[43] Of the 53 minor canons appointed between 1660 and 1776, 44 were educated at Cambridge[44] and at least 32 came from the eastern counties. From 1776 to 1795 there were seven successive appointments from Oxford colleges. With no provision for retirement many of the canons sang well into old age. Peter Hansell and Paul Whittingham both served the cathedral for more than fifty years. George Carter, George Day, John Fox, William Herne, Ephraim Megoe, Charles Millard, Charles Freeman Millard, Lynn Smear and James Williams Newton all spent more than forty years in the choir.

Lay Clerks

Whereas the minor canons derived their income from sources entirely within the church, the lay clerks carried on their own individual trades and professions. Some of their occupations are recorded: Charles Alden was a vintner, Thomas Beckwith a wig maker, and John Beckwith II a glover and breeches maker before becoming a schoolmaster; Samuel Morris was a worsted weaver, Augustine Holl a gardener, and John Swanton a twisterer. Like the canons, they were provided with

---

42. The lectures were the result of a bequest from Thomas Hall, merchant and mayor of Norwich.
    See Bloomfield III, pp. 436-7 and IV, pp. 317-8.
43. Wilson, pp. 589-90
44. Norwich Cathedral maintained a strong link with Cambridge University throughout these years.
    After 1714 the fourth prebendal stall at Norwich was annexed to St Catherine's College, Cambridge.
    See Wilson, p. 586.

a house in the precincts. Their basic salary under the statutes was eight pounds a year, plus the dividend of ten pounds from the corn rents. For much of the period one of the lay clerks acted as master of the choristers and for this he was paid an additional salary of eight pounds. Between 1704 and 1777 the position of epistoler was held by a lay clerk at the enhanced salary of eight pounds ten shillings; at other times the epistoler was a priest or deacon. Several lay clerks were paid for copying music into the choir and organ books, the principal copyists being Anthony Blagrave, James Finch, Edward Beckwith, William Cooke and Joseph Parnell. Between 1672 and 1704 one of the lay singers was granted five shillings a year for 'setting the psalms and naming the anthem'. Apart from these jobs, a few men were employed as tradesmen by the dean and chapter - Thomas Hill as carpenter, Samuel Blyth as plasterer, John Cox as upholsterer and James Cupper as bookbinder. James Finch had the job of making the choristers' gowns which were renewed every year.

In 1773 five of the lay clerks - Thomas Beckwith, John Beckwith II, Benjamin Paul, William Cooke and Samuel Harper - sent a petition to the dean and chapter requesting an increase in their salaries. As well as highlighting their financial needs the petition cited the increased musical activity that occurred during this period. They wrote:

> That the ordinary business of the church is now rendered almost double what it ever was before, by the number of verse services and anthems inserted in the weekly combinations [and that] the extraordinary new music constantly brought us to get up, requires much more time and attention than our present pay will enable us to bestow on it. We humbly beg leave to remind you that the salary to the lay clerks remains the same as when it was first established, at which time the value of money was much greater than it now is.[45]

The petition was successful and they each received a gratuity of five pounds. The payment was continued in subsequent years and extended to include all eight lay clerks with a nominal sum - usually two or three guineas - for the supernumerary. A further petition in 1790 was rejected by the chapter. In 1796, probably as a result of some squabbling, the gratuity was awarded 'in proportion to their attendance in the church'. From Christmas Day 1804 the gratuity was replaced by a flat rate of 3s. 6d. a week, with a forfeit of three pence for each unauthorised absence. Thomas Alwood, the junior subsacrist, was paid one shilling a week to keep a register of the lay clerks' attendances. In 1808, due to the improvement in the cathedral's

---

45. NRO, DCN 33/29

revenues, their basic salary of eight pounds was increased to twenty pounds. Finally, the chapter made a one-off payment of forty pounds in 1812 to be divided equally among the lay clerks 'in consideration of the high cost of provisions'.

Another instance of increased financial security for the choirmen was the formation of a lay clerks' fund which operated between 1800 and 1815. Money saved through vacancies in the choir was paid into the fund and disbursements were made to lay clerks who carried out additional duties, and to those who were unable to work because of illness. Joseph Parnell received a number of payments during his long illness and the fund paid his funeral expenses.[46]

As with the minor canons, long service also featured among the lay singers. Peter Sandley, who sang until he was around 89 years old, would have served in the choir for more than sixty years but for interruption caused by the Civil War. Thomas Mowting's position was similarly interrupted, otherwise he would have spent 53 years in the choir. Four men gave fifty or more years of uninterrupted service - Anthony Blagrave, John Beckwith II, Richard Browne and James Cupper. A further twelve lay clerks held office for more than forty years.

---

46. NRO, DCN 39/52 and 53

Ozias Thurston Linley, minor canon 1790-1816

John 'Christmas' Beckwith, lay clerk 1785-1803

i

Joseph Finch's bill for copying music, 1722
(Courtesy of Norfolk Record Office)

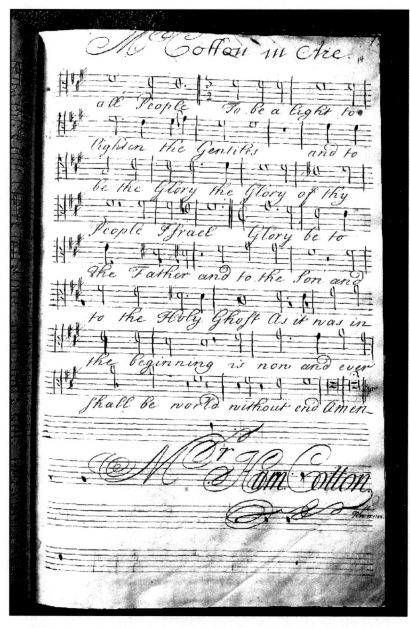

Humphrey Cotton's Service in A, copied by Joseph Finch, 1722
(Courtesy of Dean and Chapter of Norwich Cathedral)

Francis Howes, minor canon 1814-1844.
(Courtesy of Norfolk Museums Service)

John Walker, gospeller 1776-1807, and his wife.
(Courtesy of Norfolk Museums Service)

The Minor Canons

(The dates in brackets indicate the length of service in the cathedral choir.)

William Alsey (1639-1666) was initially appointed to the choir as a lay clerk on 16 January 1639, and became epistoler in June the same year. He was admonished in 1641 for being absent from services and for frequenting taverns, and reprimanded again in 1642 for living a scandalous life and neglecting the choir. In December 1644 the chapter noted that he had been long absent from the church and that his wife had died leaving two children without maintenance. In the 1649 Parliamentary Survey he had let the house assigned to him in the precincts at an annual rent of £5. He received £1 10s in 1657 out of a payment of £20 to the poor officers of the cathedral from the Trustees for the Maintenance of Ministers. He returned to the choir when it was re-formed in 1660 and on 10 June 1662, having subscribed to the Thirty-nine Articles, was admitted a minor canon. At the same time he became chaplain at St George Colegate. He was sacrist in 1663 and precentor 1664-5. He received a further reprimand for lack of attendance in 1664. His last salary was paid in 1666.

(Sources: Blomefield IV; Cornall; Matthews; Metters; W & C-H)

Charles Ames (1736-1771) was the son of a Norwich woodworker. He was educated at Norwich School and Trinity College, Cambridge, and was ordained deacon at Norwich in July 1727. In February 1736 he was appointed gospeller in the cathedral choir, becoming a minor canon in 1738. He delivered the series of Hall's Sacramental Lectures in 1733 and became a freeman of the city in the same year. He was rector of the Norwich parishes of All Saints (1737) and St Laurence (1740), vicar of Ringland (1733), rector of Hainford (1739) and vicar of Trowse with Whitlingham (1754). He died on 10 September 1771.

(AC; Blomefield IV, VIII and X; Mann Ms. 430; Millican 2; Turner)

Anthony Beck (1639-1674) joined the choir as a lay clerk on 3 September 1639. He was admonished in 1642 for neglect of his duty. In 1648 he was assigned rooms in the precincts which he shared with Redmaine Carlton, but in the 1649 Parliamentary Survey the rooms were being let to various poor people at an annual rent of £4. He received £2 10s. in 1657 from a payment of £20 to the poor officers of the cathedral from the Trustees for the Maintenance of Ministers. He resumed his place in the choir after the Interregnum and in February 1663 was ordained deacon and transferred to the clergy side. He served as precentor (1663, 1668-9), sacrist (1665-7 and 1670-3), and reader of morning prayer (1667-70),

24

and for a time in 1664 he was responsible for teaching the choristers. He composed two anthems which survive in incomplete manuscript sources. He died in 1674.
(Cornall; Mann Ms. 430; Matthews; Metters; Roast 1; W & C-H)

Thomas Beckwith (1762-1781) belonged to the Norwich family which provided six lay clerks for the cathedral choir. His father, also Thomas Beckwith, was a barber and brother of John Beckwith I. Thomas junior was educated at Norwich School and Caius College, Cambridge, and was ordained deacon at Norwich in August 1756. He was appointed minor canon on 1 January 1762 following the death of Lynn Smear. His parish appointments were Norwich St Edmund (1756-75 and 1781-1807), Eaton (1762-82), Norwich St Giles (1771-81), Bawdeswell (1774-1807) and Norwich St Martin at Palace (1781-1807). He resigned his position in the choir in 1781 upon being nominated to St Martin at Palace. He died on 30 September 1807, aged 72.
(AC; G. Mag. 1807; Mann Ms. 430; Turner)

William Bentham (1720-1731) came from Ely and was educated at St John's College, Cambridge. He was ordained in 1718 and appointed minor canon in January 1720. He was granted a lease of the Norwich parishes of St James and St Paul, Pockthorpe in 1720 which he resigned in June 1725 upon being nominated to the vicarage at Catton. However, although the chapter voted 4 to 2 in favour of the appointment, the dean refused the presentation and Bentham remained at Pockthorpe. He was additionally parish chaplain at St Giles' and St Gregory's, and rector of Tasburgh. He was precentor 1727-31 and preached the Good Friday sermon in the cathedral in 1728. He died on 27 February 1731, aged 37.
(AC; Blomefield IV and V; Goodman, part 1, p.4)

John Blagrave (1702-1712) came from a Norwich musical family, his father Anthony and elder brother Richard both being cathedral lay clerks. John was baptized on 1 January 1679. He was admitted to the choir as a minor canon in 1702 and presented to the benefice of Eaton in 1705. On 8 January 1712 he was admonished by the dean, Humphrey Prideaux, for frequenting taverns and alehouses. He was given a second admonition on 13 February for spending all afternoon at the Maid's Head and then coming to the precincts 'exceedingly drunk ... to the dishonour of his function and the scandal of this church'. On 15 March he was arrested for debt and conveyed to the city prison after becoming senseless at a notorious bawdy house where he was observed in the company of

two wenches and in a posture with one of them which was both 'immodest and suspicious'. This was all too much for the dean who obtained written testimony from four witnesses to Blagrave's misconduct and then summoned him to appear on 24 March and expelled him from the cathedral. A few years later Blagrave was advertising his services as a teacher of grammar, writing and arithmetic. He died in August 1727 at the age of 48.
(Blomefield IV; Mann Ms. 430)

Richard Bracket (c.1606-1634) was from Wreningham, Norfolk. He was educated at Norwich School and Caius College, Cambridge, and was ordained at Norwich in 1602. He held curacies at Ashwellthorpe and Intwood, and was appointed minor canon around 1606. He was rector of St Augustine's Norwich from 1617: Blomefield mentions a brass to his memory in the nave. He died on 29 December 1634.
(AC; Blomefield IV; Cornall)

John Brooke (1732-1747) came from Nacton, Suffolk. After graduating LLB from Pembroke College, Cambridge in 1732 he was admitted to the cathedral choir in the position of gospeller, becoming a full minor canon in 1736. He was appointed to the Norwich benefices of St Augustine (1733), St Peter Southgate (1738) and St Etheldreda (1746), and to Colney (1743), all of which he held for the rest of his life. He was at some time curate at St John Timberhill, rector of Gosbeck and Bucklesham in Suffolk, and chaplain to the garrison at Quebec. He delivered the series of Hall's Sacremental Lectures in 1735 and 1743. At the cathedral he preached the Good Friday sermon in 1737 and was reader of morning prayer in 1745. In March 1747 he was called three times by the dean, who had affixed notices to the effect on the cathedral doors, to explain his absence from the choir and on failing to appear on any occasion he was dismissed for 'deserting the duty of his office'. He remained with his parishes and died at Colney on 21 January 1789. His wife, who was an authoress, died two days later.
(AC; Blomefield IV and V; G. Mag. 1789; Turner)

John Browne (1668-1670) was admitted minor canon on probation at Midsummer 1668 and confirmed in the position the following October. He officiated as sacrist in 1669 and 1670. He was described as 'late' in February 1671 when his house in the precincts was assigned to John Parris. He may have been the same John Browne who was born at Tacolneston, Norfolk, educated at Caius College, Cambridge,

and ordained at Norwich in 1644.
(AC)

Michael Browne (1782-1811) came from Worcester and graduated from New College, Oxford in 1780. He was admitted to the office of minor canon in January 1782 and presented to the parishes of Eaton and Norwich St Gregory, both of which he resigned in 1786 in favour of the more lucrative livings of Norwich St Giles and Worstead. In June 1811 the chapter ordered that the considerable sum of one hundred pounds 'be subscribed for the benefit of the Revd. Mr Browne or his family'. He died on 28 July 1811, aged 53. His daughter, Charlotte Elizabeth Tonna, was an evangelical Protestant writer and novelist: she edited *The Christian Lady's Magazine* and *The Protestant Magazine*.
(AO; Mann Ms. 430; NC, 13 February 1841; Turner)

Samuel Bull (1691-1705) from Norwich was educated at Corpus Christi College, Cambridge. He was admitted as a probationer minor canon in November 1691 and given a full place in September 1693. In 1699 he was appointed vicar of Eaton but he resigned his position, and his place in the choir, in 1705 upon being appointed vicar of Westhall, Suffolk. He was subsequently presented to the nearby rectories of Frostenden and Brampton.
(AC; Blomefield IV)

Peter Burgess (1686-1723). Born at Norwich, the son of a weaver, he attended Pembroke College, Cambridge. He became gospeller in 1686 and minor canon in 1687, and was granted a lease for life of the rectory of St Martin at Coslany, Norwich. At the cathedral he was sacrist from 1692 to 1696, and was then precentor for 27 years until his death. He was admonished in 1702 for inviting John Stukeley to baptize his child in the cathedral, knowing that Stukeley had been expelled from the church. The chapter paid him for binding the choirboys' books in 1719 and for preaching the Rogation sermon in 1721. He was vicar of Scarning and rector of Whinburgh. He was buried on 5 April 1723.
(AC; Blomefield X; Mann Ms. 430)

Philip Burroughs (1715-1718) came from London and attended Wadham College, Oxford. He seems to have been ill prepared for his job as a minor canon to which he was appointed, apparently from a rural curacy, in May 1715. The Chapter Book records that he was made to promise 'that I will, under a skilful master, learn to sing and continue diligently to improve myself herein under his directions'. Later the same year he was presented to the livings of Lakenham and Catton. In 1718 he went to Whitlingham to drink a bowl of punch with 'two idle and loose fellows'. On his return he was thrown from his horse in Conesford Street and broke his skull from which he died three days later.

(AO; Blomefield IV and X; DCN 33/5 and 115/3)

George Carter (1816-1860) was born at Oxford in 1792 and was a chorister at Magdalen College from 1802 to 1807. He graduated from Christ Church in 1813, and was a singing clerk there from 1813 to 1815, and chaplain of New College from 1815 to 1818. He was appointed minor canon at Norwich in August 1816 in place of Ozias Linley and in the same year was presented to the benefices of Trowse and Lakenham, parishes which he served for the rest of his life. He was precentor from 1831 to 1844 and during these years he procured a good deal of new music for the choir. The chapter agreed to augment his precentor's salary by £10 a year as he was residing away from the cathedral at Lakenham Terrace. Unlike the other minor canons, who were meted out several dean and chapter livings, George Carter held only one additional benefice, that of Bawburgh from 1829. As early as 1817 he took boarding pupils between the ages of seven and fourteen, offering an education in the classics in return for a fee of one hundred guineas a year. He continued to instruct pupils until at least 1855, though it may have been a sign of the difficult times that his fees dropped to eighty guineas in 1822 and fifty guineas (for the under 12s) in 1827. He was president of the Norwich Public Library when it moved to new premises in 1837. He died of bronchitis on 26 February 1860, aged 67, having been a minor canon for 43 years. Memorials were erected at both Trowse and Lakenham to mark his long service to those parishes.

(AO; Bloxam; Mann Ms. 431; NC, 3 March 1860 and 3 May 1862)

John Connould (1670-1691) came from Laxfield, Suffolk, and attended Trinity College, Cambridge. He was initially admitted to the choir as lay clerk and epistoler in June 1670, but was appointed minor canon upon becoming ordained in October 1670. He was gospeller (1671-72 and 1674-80), precentor (1673) and sacrist (1681-91). He preached the Good Friday sermon in the cathedral in 1691. He held the livings of Catton (1672), Catfield (1680) and the Norwich parishes of St Simon and St Jude (1683) and St Stephen (1683). In 1691 he was given two admonitions by the dean and chapter for not reading the prayer for the King. Connould had refused to take the oath of allegiance to King William, having previously done so to King James II who was still living. On receiving a third admonition he was expelled from the choir. However, he was not deprived of his parishes which he continued to serve until his death in May 1708, aged 62. Connould became noted for his friendship with Thomas Grantham, a controversial Baptist leader. Grantham had stirred up opposition in Norwich through his defiance of the doctrine of the Church of England, and when he died Connould (in order to prevent defilement of the corpse) allowed his body to be buried inside the west door of St Stephen's church. Connould composed eight anthems, two service settings and some chants for use at the cathedral: these survive in manuscript form but are all incomplete in some way. A slab to his memory is in the chancel floor at St Stephen's.

(AC; Jewson; Roast 1)

John Cornwall (1689-1690) came from Norwich and was educated at Hertford School and Peterhouse College, Cambridge. He was paid for serving as a minor canon for one year to Michaelmas 1690 but was not formally admitted to the choir.

(AC)

George Day (1816-1864) was born at Norwich in the parish of St Giles, the son of a worsted weaver. He graduated from Corpus Christi College, Cambridge and was ordained deacon at Norwich in December 1815. He was appointed minor canon in November 1816 in place of James Williams Newton, and was immediately presented to the parishes of Sprowston and Great Plumstead. In 1817 he resigned these parishes in favour of Eaton and Barton Bendish, both of which he held until his death. He was also perpetual curate of Hemblington (1826) and St Peter Parmentergate, Norwich (1824). At the cathedral he was reader of morning prayer for the unusually long period of thirty years from 1818 to 1848. He was appointed by Norwich Corporation to preach Hall's Sacramental Lectures in 1825/6. A H Mann, who was a cathedral chorister during George Day's later years, remembered him as 'a short stout man, and we always referred to him as "old Johnny Day". His voice was more like a nutmeg grater than anything I ever remember. It had the ordinary compass of a most ordinary tenor'. None the less, this ordinary tenor did a good deal of singing. As well as his duties in the cathedral choir he was a long-serving member of Norwich Choral Society, and he sang in the chorus at every Norwich Triennial Musical Festival from its inception in 1824 until 1860. He died on 28 December 1864 aged 73, after 48 years as a minor canon. A memorial at Eaton records his long service to that parish. His son, Lewis Framingham Day, was organist at the parish church at Burton on Trent for nearly

60 years.
(AC; Mann Ms. 431; NC, 8 November 1856; Turner)

Richard Deere (1729-1737) was from Cambridgeshire and attended Jesus College, Cambridge. He became gospeller in 1729 and minor canon in 1731. He was presented to the parish of St John de Sepulchre in 1730. In June 1734 he was admonished for his poor attendance in the choir. He died at the age of 31 on 23 July 1737 and was buried in the cathedral. A memorial was prepared with an inscription written by his tutor at Cambridge, but it was not allowed to be displayed because it suggested that he deserved a higher position than that of minor canon.
(AC; Blomefield IV; Mann Ms. 431)

Peter Delahaye (1679-1687). Also styled as Peter de la Haye, this musician was from Caen, Normandy. He was admitted minor canon in 1679 and appointed sacrist 1681-1687. He was presented to the parish of Catton in 1681, and was sometime rector of St Augustine's, Norwich. He died on 16 October 1687.
(AC; Blomefield IV)

William Dilke (1682) - also spelt Delke - was ordained at Norwich in July 1681. He made a number of appearances in the choir in 1682 in the place of a minor canon for which he was paid £5, but he received no formal appointment. He became rector of Bixley (1690) and Necton (1693). He died in 1718.
(AC; Blomefield V and VI)

William Fitt Drake (1811-1836) was born in Norwich, the son of a manufacturer, and educated at Norwich School and Corpus Christi College, Cambridge. He was ordained at Norwich in 1810 and was sworn in as a minor canon in September 1811 in place of Michael Browne. He was immediately presented to the Norwich parishes of St Stephen and St John Timberhill, followed by Arminghall (1813), Stoke Holy Cross (1814) and Norwich St Gregory (1831). In December 1818 he was appointed by the dean and chapter to be chapter librarian at an annual salary of £10, and he shared forty guineas with John Kitson (the chapter clerk) for arranging the library and making a new catalogue. Between around 1820 and 1836 he was involved with a number of local organisations: treasurer for many years to the Institution for the Indigent Blind; president of the Public Library; joint secretary and treasurer to the Trustees of the Charity Schools; committee member of the Norfolk and Norwich Literary Institution; joint treasurer to the Triennial Musical

30

Musical Festivals of 1827, 1830 and 1833; and joint honorary auditor to the Norfolk and Norwich Hospital in 1835 and 1836. He was examining chaplain to Bishop Bathurst from 1829 to 1836, and was chaplain to several mayors. He resigned his office of minor canon on 26 January 1836 upon being presented to the living of West Halton, Lincolnshire. The parishioners of St Stephen's gave him a tea service in recognition of his twenty-five years as their vicar. He was rector of West Halton for the rest of his life, although following his wife's death in 1860 he returned to live in Norwich and began making appearances at meetings in the city from around 1868. He died at his house in the precincts on 5 May 1874 at the age of 87.

(AC; Clergy List 1873; Eade p. 198; NC various; Turner)

Thomas Dunch (1715-1719) was from Cambridgeshire and attended Corpus Christi College, Cambridge. He was admitted gospeller in January 1705 but immediately given leave of absence to continue his studies at Cambridge with no pay until he took up residence in Norwich. He was ordained in 1708 and returned to Norwich as gospeller in September 1715, becoming a full minor canon in October 1718. He was rector of Antingham (1710-18) and of Bergh Apton (1717-19). He died on 26 December 1719.

(AC; Blomefield IV, VIII and X)

Henry Fish (1712-1714) from Kings Lynn went to Christ's College, Cambridge and was ordained at Norwich in 1709. He was appointed gospeller in February 1712 and minor canon soon after but resigned in April 1714. He held a number of benefices - Irstead (1711), Scottow (1713), Middleton (1722) and Walpole (1726) - and was chaplain to the Earl of Kinnoull. His sermon entitled *The period of human life* was published in 1738.

(AC; BL)

Francis Folchier (1690-1715) received a specially-conferred degree at Cambridge in 1690. In the same year he replaced John Cornwall as minor canon though his position was not confirmed until October 1691. He was presented to the benefices of Catton (1690) and Lakenham (1692). He served as precentor (1703-4) and sacrist (1696 and 1705-7), and was paid one pound for preaching the Good Friday sermon in 1712. In May 1715 he was made to confess to the dean that he had fathered a child with his servant, Dorothy Bernard, and had abused Anne Brown, his former servant. Folchier immediately resigned from the choir, and later the same year he was deprived of his livings at Catton and Lakenham. He was replaced in all his

positions by Philip Burroughs.
(AC)

Pexall Forster (1718-1719) was born in 1693 at Durham, the son of a clergyman. He obtained a BA from Lincoln College, Oxford and MA from King's College, Cambridge. In June 1718 he was appointed a supernumerary minor canon (the only time during this period that such an appointment was made) and reader of morning prayer until a place of gospeller or minor canon became available. He was admitted gospeller in October 1718 in place of Thomas Dunch, and precentor in January 1719, and was given the livings of Lakenham and Norwich St James. He died on 4 October 1719 aged 26 without becoming a full minor canon.
(AC; AO; Blomefield IV)

John Fox (1714-1758). The minute recording the admission of John Fox as a minor canon is dated April 1714. He was born at Holt and attended Clare College, Cambridge. He was ordained deacon at Lincoln (1712) and priest at Norwich (1714), and was appointed to the benefices at Hemblington, Surlingham and Lakenham. In 1725 Gilbert Pickering resigned the living at Catton, and Fox was nominated by the dean to replace him, but the chapter voted by 4 to 2 in favour of William Bentham. The dean, however, refused to approve the presentation of Bentham, and Fox became vicar of Catton which he held with Lakenham for the rest of his life. At the cathedral he was librarian from 1729, and was sacrist from 1729 until at least 1749. He died on 5 December 1758 in his seventieth year, having completed more than 44 years in the choir.
(AC; Blomefield IV, V and X; NM, 9 December 1758)

William Fugill (1598-after 1646) was ordained at Norwich in 1598 after attending Peterhouse College, Cambridge and was appointed minor canon at the cathedral and vicar of Catton. He was admonished by the dean and chapter in 1621 and 1625 for neglecting his duties, and was warned about his drunkenness in 1627. He was rector of St George Tombland from 1604 and at the episcopal visitation of 1627 he was again found to be neglecting parochial duties and frequenting alehouses. He was still receiving his minor canon's salary in 1646 although choral services in the cathedral had ceased by that time. He was not reappointed to the choir at the Restoration and probably died during the Interregnum.
(AC; Blomefield IV and X; Cornall; DCN 10/2/1; Houlbrooke p. 519; W & C-H)

Richard Greene (1665). This singer was paid a half-year's salary as a minor canon in 1665 though he was not formally appointed to the position.

Peter Hansell (1786-1841) was born at Reading. He was a chorister at Magdalen College, Oxford before graduating there in 1785, and was admitted minor canon at Norwich in 1786 following the death of Ephraim Megoe. He was precentor from 1811 to 1831. The dean and chapter licensed him to the perpetual curacies of two poor Norwich parishes in 1788, St John de Sepulchre and St Martin at Oak, which he served for 53 years and 43 years respectively. Other preferments were Norwich St Augustine (1790), Arminghall (1792), Catton (1795) and Worstead (1811). In 1794 he married Rebecca Garland, daughter of the cathedral organist. Kitton described him as a clergyman of the old school, with powdered hair and black dress coat and boots, and possessing a sonorous bass voice. For several years he was associated with the Institution for the Indigent Blind, acting as their chairman and vice-president. In June 1836 the chapter presented him with a theological work to the value of ten pounds to mark his fiftieth year as a minor canon. He died on 9 January 1841 at the age of 76 and was interred in the south transept of the cathedral. On the Sunday after his funeral Canon Wodehouse preached a sermon proclaiming his qualities as a priest and pastor: the sermon was published by request. More than 60 years later, in October 1908, two bells were added to the ring at St John de Sepulchre as a memorial to Peter Hansell's long ministry to the parish.
(AO; Kitton p. 37; NC, 6 February 1841 and 24 October 1908; Turner)

Henry Harington (1777-1790). Two musicians of this name, both known as Dr Henry Harington, flourished during the eighteenth century. Harington senior was a doctor of medicine with a practice at Wells, Somerset; his son was a doctor of divinity who, after graduating from Queen's College, Oxford was admitted to the office of epistoler at Norwich Cathedral in 1777. Harington junior remained in Norwich for the rest of his life. In 1782 he resigned as epistoler and was simultaneously appointed a minor canon. His parishes included Westhall, Suffolk, Great Plumstead and Arminghall (all presented in 1779), Hainford (1791) and Norwich St George Colegate (1785). In addition he was elected by the parishioners of St Peter Mancroft to be their assistant minister in 1781. He was honorary auditor to the Norfolk and Norwich Hospital in 1785/86, and was steward at the charity service for the hospital held at the cathedral in 1786. He resigned his minor canonry in February 1790 and was replaced by Ozias Linley. A number of compositions attributed to Henry Harington or Dr Harington are almost certainly by Harington senior, but a work entitled *Euterpe, or remarks on the* *use and abuse of music* published in 1778 is by the Norwich Harington. In it he attacks modern music and recommends composers to follow the ways of 'the immortal Handel'. Chambers believed he also edited *Nugae Antiquae* from the papers of his ancestor Sir John Harington, the poet. He died on the 25 December 1791 at the age of 36. A tablet to his memory is at St Peter Mancroft.

(AO; Chambers p. 938; Eade p.196; Roast 1; Turner)

Cropley Hatch (1748-1755) was from Norfolk. He attended Corpus Christi College, Cambridge and was ordained deacon at Norwich in 1744. The Chapter Book does not record his appointment as a minor canon but it probably occurred in June 1748. On 2 August 1755 he appeared before the dean and was admonished for leaving his lodgings and taking up residence at the Gatehouse public house. A second admonition was given two days later, and being convinced that he had no intention of returning to his lodgings the dean called him a third time and expelled him from the cathedral. What happened to him after that is not known. He was buried on 5 March 1763.

(AC; Mann Ms. 431)

William Herbert (1672-1673). After attending Trinity College, Cambridge he was admitted epistoler in June 1672 and minor canon upon his ordination in September of that year. For a time he was reader of morning prayer. He died in 1673 and the dean and chapter gave two pounds towards his funeral.

(AC)

William Herne (1727-1775). His father, also William Herne, was rector of St George Colegate, Norwich from 1715 to 1745. William junior was born at Norwich and educated at Norwich School and Caius College, Cambridge. He was ordained deacon at Oxford in 1722 and priest at Norwich in 1724, and he served as curate to his father. In March 1727 he was appointed minor canon at the cathedral, and the Chapter Book records that he was also deputy precentor in 1736 and precentor in 1761. In 1728 he delivered the series of Hall's Sacramental Lectures for the Norwich Corporation. He was presented to the parishes of Horningtoft (1728), Hemblington (1729), Norwich St James and St Paul (1735), Garveston (1744) and Alderford with Attlebridge (1762), and he held them all into his old age whilst still serving the cathedral as senior minor canon and having the additional duties of sacrist and librarian from 1762. He died at his home in the precincts on 25 November 1775 at the age of 76. He had been a minor canon for over 48 years.

(AC; Blomefield IV; Mann Ms. 431; Turner)

Thomas Horne (1626/7-c.1662) was initially admitted to the cathedral choir as a singing man around 1626 and he became a minor canon in April 1633. He acted as sacrist for two periods. In 1646 he was assigned chambers in the cloisters, but at the time of the 1649 Parliamentary Survey he had let them at £2 a year. He received £2 in 1657 out of a payment of £20 by the Trustees for the Maintenance of Ministers for the poor officers of the cathedral. He was one of only two minor canons to resume his position in the choir in 1660. He was paid half his salary for the year to Michaelmas 1662 and he died sometime before May 1663 when his house was assigned to Nicholas Bagley.
(Cornall; Matthews; Metters; W&C-H)

Thomas Housden (1670-1672) studied at King's College, Cambridge and was admitted minor canon in January 1671 though he probably joined the choir at Michaelmas 1670. In December 1671 he was admonished for frequent drunkenness and for this, and for deserting the choir, he was expelled in June 1672.
(AC)

Francis Howes (1814-1844) was descended from a minor gentry family who had lived in the Wymondham area since the middle ages. He was the son of the Reverend Thomas Howes and was born at Morningthorpe on 29 February 1776. He attended the Norwich School under Dr Parr and graduated from Trinity College, Cambridge in 1798. He was ordained in 1800 and was appointed to the parishes of Shillington, Bedfordshire in 1801, Wickham Skeith, Suffolk in 1809, and Buckenham with Hassingham, Norfolk in 1811. In November 1814 he was admitted minor canon at Norwich in place of Charles Millard and given the dean and chapter benefices of Norwich St George Colegate and Bawburgh. For two years he was reader of morning prayer. His other livings were Alderford with Attlebridge (1826) and Framingham Pigot (1829). Howes was a classical scholar and in addition to his clerical and musical duties he published a number of learned works, among them *Miscellaneous Poetical Translations* (1806), *The Satires of A Persius Flaccus* (1809), and *The Epodes and Secular Ode of Horace* (1841). In 1830 he translated the text of a composition by Mozart, known in English as *The Dedication of the Temple*, which was performed at the Norwich Triennial Musical Festival that year. When a memorial to Bishop Bathurst was placed in the cathedral in 1841 it bore a Latin inscription written by Howes who was described as the bishop's 'faithful chaplain and friend'. Francis Howes died at his house in the precincts on 26 March 1844 aged 68 and was buried in the cathedral cloisters. His entire and

undisturbed library of 3000 volumes was sold at auction.
(AC; G. Mag. 1844; NC, 27 November 1841 and 17 August 1844; ODNB; Turner; Saunders)

Richard Hughes (1681-1689) came from Dorset and graduated from All Souls' College, Oxford in 1681. He was formally admitted as a minor canon in July 1682 but was paid from Michaelmas 1681. His last salary was paid in 1689. Blomefield records a memorial in the cathedral giving the date of his death as 8 August 1698.
(AO; Blomefield IV)

Ozias Thurston Linley (1790-1816) was a member of one of the best-known families of English musicians active during the second half of the eighteenth century. His father was Thomas Linley, the stage composer and joint director of the Drury Lane Theatre. His brothers Thomas junior and William were both minor composers, and his three sisters were singers. Ozias Linley was born at Bath in August 1765 and received musical tuition from Sir William Herschel, the astronomer, who was organist at the Octagon Chapel in Bath, He graduated from Corpus Christi College, Oxford in 1789, took holy orders, and was admitted minor canon at Norwich on 20 March 1790. He held several local benefices, all of them dean and chapter livings, at Norwich St George Colegate (1790), Sprowston, Great Plumstead and Bawburgh (1795), Stoke Holy Cross (1807) and Trowse with Lakenham (1814). He was reader of morning prayer from 1797 to 1808. He resigned his positions in 1816 upon being appointed organist-fellow at Dulwich College where his duties required him to play the chapel organ on Sundays and to instruct the children in music. He returned to Norwich in 1827 to attend the Triennial Musical Festival at which a composition by his father was performed. He died at Dulwich in March 1831 at the age of 65 and was the last person to be buried in the college chapel. Ozias Linley was a capable composer who wrote several works for the church. His known compositions comprise an anthem, two services, two settings of the morning canticles, and some metrical psalm tunes and chants. Some of these pieces were copied into contemporary choirbooks at Norwich Cathedral. He was also a scholarly man, prone to eccentric behaviour and possessed of a fertile imagination. A younger colleague at Dulwich, the Reverend John Sinclair, in a publication of his own reminiscences recalled some of Linley's peculiar ways, most notably his spurious assertion (described in detail) of how Handel paid a visit to Norwich Cathedral one Sunday and played the organ after morning service. Another story tells of how Linley would give his chambermaid the texts of his sermons with which to light the fire.
(AO; Black; G. Mag. 1831; NC, 22 September 1827; Roast 1 and 4; Sinclair; Turner)

Thomas Manlove (1723-1736) was born in 1698 at Longstanton, Cambridgeshire where his father was vicar. After graduating from Emmanuel College, Cambridge he was ordained and appointed gospeller and reader of morning prayer at Norwich in June 1723. He was chosen to deliver the series of Hall's Sacramental Lectures in 1724. The following year the chapter paid him for transcribing the cathedral's Statutes and Articles of Visitation. He was admitted to a full minor canon's place in December 1726 on the death of John Paul. He held the benefices of the Norwich parishes of St John Timberhill and St James with St Paul, and was vicar of Surlingham from 1725 to 1731. He preached the Good Friday sermon in the cathedral in 1731 and the Rogation sermon in 1724 and 1734. He was also appointed vicar of St Stephen's (1729), assistant minister at St Peter Mancroft (1735) and rector of Caistor St Edmund with Markshall. For a reason that is not clear he resigned his place in the cathedral choir in February 1736. He died on 9 September 1746.

(AC; Blomefield IV and V; NG, 13 September 1746)

Ephraim Megoe (1737-1786) served in the choir for nearly half a century. He came from Norwich and attended Corpus Christi College, Cambridge. Following ordination at Norwich he became gospeller in 1737 and minor canon in 1739. He gave the series of Hall's Sacramental Lectures in 1740 and preached the Good Friday sermon in the cathedral in 1771. He was usher (second master) at Norwich Grammar School from Ladyday 1746 to Christmas 1747. His parishes were St John de Sepulchre (1738) and St Martin at Oak (1743) in Norwich, Spexhall, Suffolk (1751) and Worstead (1762), all of which he held until his death at the age of 74 on 14 June 1786. He was buried in the cathedral.

(AC; Blomefield IV; Mann Ms. 432; Saunders; Turner)

William Merrick (1610-c.1638) is first mentioned as gospeller in 1610.He became a minor canon in 1613 and was chosen as sacrist and precentor at various times until 1638. In 1614 he was admonished for neglecting his duties and for leaving the service before prayers were ended. He was paid £9 by the chapter for copying music into the choirbooks in 1615.

(Cornall; W & C-H)

Charles Millard (1771-1814) was born at Gloucester in 1748. He was a chorister at Magdalen College, Oxford between 1761 and 1767, and in 1763 he sang a duet with the Italian prima donna Giulia Frasi at a music meeting in Gloucester. He developed a pure tenor voice and on graduating from Magdalen College he was appointed to a minor canon's place at Norwich in December 1771 at the age of 23. He was precentor from 1776 to 1811, and was chaplain to Bishop George Horne whom he attended in his last hours. He became chancellor of the diocese in 1809. He preached the Good Friday sermon on five occasions and gave the Anniversary Sermon on behalf of the Norfolk and Norwich Hospital in 1809. He was presented to the parishes of Trowse with Lakenham (1772), Hemblington (1775), St John Timberhill and St Martin at Palace, Norwich and Stoke Holy Cross (1776) and Taverham (1793). The nature of these preferments meant that by the 1780s Millard's income was higher by a margin than those of his fellow minor canons. For several years he was one of the proprietors of the Theatre Royal, and he served as vice-president of the Norwich Public Library. A chant of his composition occurs in Beckwith's published collection of 1808. He died on 6 November 1814 aged 66 and a memorial stone was erected at Old Lakenham church.

(AO; Bloxham; DCN 33/21; Eshleman; Howard; Mann Ms. 432; NC, 10 September 1814; Roast 3; Turner)

Charles Freeman Millard (1807-1849) was the eldest son of the foregoing. Born at Norwich in 1774 he graduated from Pembroke College, Cambridge and was ordained in 1798. From 1802 to 1807 he was usher (second master) at Norwich Grammar School. In November 1807 he was appointed gospeller in the cathedral choir and he remained in that position for the rest of his life, apparently shunning the usual advancement to a full minor canon's place with its enhanced salary. From 1808 to 1815 he was reader of morning prayer. He was presented to the livings of Didlington with Colveston (1802), Hickling (1803), Norwich St Martin at Palace and Henly, Suffolk (1807), Norwich St Giles (1811), and finally to one of the chapter's best livings at Sedgeford (1831) where he subsequently built a new vicarage. In 1837 he was asked by Dean Pellew to modify his 'forte piano mode of chanting and reading ... unexpectedly loud at intervals as to cause the congregation to look up, and again so piano as to render it difficult to make the responses correctly ... which excites in the less serious portion of the congregation feelings different from those which you would wish them to entertain'. Millard was involved with several institutions in the city: from at least 1815 until 1839 he was chaplain to the Norwich gaol, giving each prisoner one shilling on Christmas Eve; he was the mayor's chaplain in 1821; he was joint secretary to the Norfolk and Norwich Magdalen; and treasurer to both the Norwich Charity Schools and the Norwich Female Friendly Society. At the Triennial Musical Festivals of 1824 and

1827 he played double bass in the orchestra. He died at his house in the precincts on 2 June 1849 at the age of 74, and was buried in the cathedral cloisters. Among his possessions sold at auction were two superior violins, a Broadwood cottage piano, a library of 500 books and an extensive collection of wine.

(AC; DCN 120/2J/5; NC, 23 June 1849; Saunders; Turner; Wilson)

Gawen Nash (1673-1691). After graduating from Trinity College, Cambridge he was ordained at Norwich and admitted minor canon in July 1673. He was sacrist 1674-78 and reader of morning prayer 1674-75. He was appointed vicar of Little Melton (where his father had been incumbent during the Interregnum), rector of Belaugh and curate of Norwich St George Tombland. In 1691 he was expelled from the choir and deprived of his benefices for refusing to take the oath of allegiance to King William and Queen Mary, believing that his former oath to King James must be honoured as long as he lived. He died in December 1706. Blomefield refers to a memorial in the churchyard at St George Tombland.

(AC; Blomefield IV and V; Overton)

Samuel Newman (1660-1679) was one of the first new appointments to the choir when it was re-formed after the Interregnum. He was initially admitted as a lay clerk in December 1660 and served as epistoler in 1661 and 1662. On 2 September 1662 he acknowledged the Thirty-nine Articles, and took the oaths of supremacy and allegiance, and became a minor canon. He was sacrist (1663), gospeller (1664) and epistoler (1671-72), and was paid for getting the choirbooks bound in 1664. He remained in the choir until his death in 1679.

James Williams Newton (1776-1817) was born in Oxfordshire in 1740. He attended Christ's Hospital and graduated from Pembroke College, Cambridge in 1762. He was ordained at Norwich in 1763 and appointed curate at Great Yarmouth the same year. He served subsequent curacies at the Suffolk parishes of Wrentham (1766) and Dennington (1772). In May 1776 he was admitted minor canon at Norwich and presented to the dean and chapter livings of Norwich St James and St Paul, Alderford with Attlebridge, and Westhall, Suffolk. He was chapter librarian from 1781 and was paid one guinea in 1790 for making a catalogue of the books. He preached the Good Friday sermon on five occasions. In 1778 he became usher (second master) at Norwich Grammar School and was effectively in charge for a time while the school was without a headmaster. He resigned as usher at Christmas 1779 to run his own private school which he

conducted until he was reappointed to the ushership in 1788. His second spell at the school lasted until 1802. He became rector of Norwich St George Colegate in 1795 and of Hemblington in 1814. In 1817 he resigned his place as a minor canon on account of his age and infirmity, but he was allowed to stay in his rectory at Hemblington with the assistance of a curate 'in consideration of his long and faithful services in the church'. He died on 30 January 1826 at the age of 85 and was buried at the cathedral. A stone to his memory is in the north walk of the cloisters. Newton published two collections of music during his lifetime. *Six Sonatas* for flutes or violins appeared in 1766 when he was twenty five years old. He inscribed the work 'Opera Prima', no doubt intending further volumes to follow. In 1775 he published a collection of psalm tunes and anthems entitled *Psalmody Improved* which he intended to be useful to country choirs. It seems that no further music followed these early publications, but in 1805 he produced *A New and Easy Introduction to the Hebrew Language*, a small pocket book containing illustrated examples of the Hebrew alphabet and rules for pronunciation and grammar.
(AC; Chambers; Mann Ms. 432; Roast 1; Saunders)

William Newton (1674-1681) came from Maidstone, Kent. After graduating from Magdalen College, Cambridge he was ordained at Norwich and appointed minor canon in November 1674. He officiated as sacrist (1679-80) and reader of morning prayer (1677-79). He died in 1681.
(AC)

Thomas Ottway (1728-1732). Born at Middleton, Westmorland and educated at Sedburgh School and Christ's College, Cambridge, Ottway was admitted gospeller in June 1728 and minor canon in January 1729. He was appointed to the Norwich parishes of St Paul and St James in April 1729 and to St Augustine's in 1730. He died on 31 July 1732 aged 28. A memorial is recorded in Blomefield.
(AC; Blomefield IV)

Stephen Painter (1674-1678) was born at Manchester in 1647. He graduated from Trinity College, Cambridge and was ordained at Norwich and admitted minor canon in May 1674. During his time in the choir he acted in the additional capacity of epistoler as that position had been unfilled since the Restoration. He was reader of morning prayer 1675-77, and preached both the Good Friday and Rogation sermons in 1678. He left the choir in July 1678 upon being appointed rector at the church of St Michael at Plea. He died on 13 July 1689 and was buried in the chancel

at St Michael at Plea. Blomefield records a memorial there.
(AC; Blomefirld IV)

John Parris (1670-1696) attended Trinity College, Cambridge. He was admitted to the choir at Norwich in 1670. He was precentor and reader of morning prayer 1671-72, gospeller 1673, and precentor again 1674-96. He was presented to the livings of Norwich St Peter Southgate in 1671, Easton in 1672 and Stoke Holy Cross in 1673. In 1685, as a result of his diligent attendance and his care in taking a record of absentees from the choir, he was allowed to have the fines arising from the absences. He died in 1696.
(AC; Blomefield IV)

John Paul (1706-1726) was the son of a Norwich baker. He was educated at Norwich School and Caius College, Cambridge, and ordained at Norwich in 1704. In 1705 he was Master of Yarmouth Grammar School, and was appointed minor canon in August 1706. He was presented to the Norwich rectories of St James and St Paul (1706) and St Giles and St Gregory (1714), and was rector of Little Moulton (1720-25). He was the first keeper of the dean and chapter library, and he preached the Good Friday sermon in 1711 and the Rogation sermon in 1711, 1712 and 1726. He died on 28 September 1726 aged 46 and was buried at St Etheldreda's church where a memorial was placed.
(AC; Blomefield IV and V)

Gilbert Pickering (1712-1727) came from Norwich and after graduating from Corpus Christi College, Cambridge he returned to Norwich for his ordination. He was admitted gospeller in 1712 and minor canon in 1715. He served the parishes of Norwich St James and St Paul (1715), Catton (1718), Hemblington (1719), Braydeston (1724) and Strumpshaw (1724).He was precentor 1723-26. On 26 January 1727 Pickering was admonished by the dean for his lack of attendance at cathedral services (which Pickering blamed on the demands of his parishes in the county) and for not wearing the hood proper to his degree (as required by the statutes). The following day he was summoned again and admonished for his rude and insolent behaviour towards the dean after his previous reprimand. Pickering immediately resigned from the choir, thereby avoiding a third admonition and possible expulsion.
(AC; Blomefield IV and V)

William Rampley (1666-1668) from Walsham-le-Willows in Suffolk was educated at Caius College, Cambridge and ordained at Norwich in 1662. He was appointed rector of Gunthorpe and Bale in 1663, and in 1666 was admitted minor canon and precentor at the cathedral. He was reader of morning prayer in 1667 and the same year was granted a lease for 21 years of the parish of St Peter Parmentergate. He suffered some abuses from another minor canon, Christopher Stinnet, about which he complained to the dean who gave Stinnet an admonition. Rampley's last salary was paid at Christmas 1668.
(AC)

Joseph Ransome (1670) spent a brief period in the choir. Originally from Chesterton in Cambridgeshire he graduated from Pembroke College, Cambridge. He sang as a probationary minor canon for six months in 1670 and acted as reader of morning prayer for nine months, but apparently received no formal appointment. He was licensed to teach grammar in 1673, and was rector of Bradfield from 1677 to 1709. Blomefield refers to a memorial to his wife in the cathedral.
(AC; Blomefield IV and XI)

Charles Ray (1731-1739). Ray was from Norfolk and he attended Corpus Christi College, Cambridge. He was ordained at Norwich in June 1731 and was admitted to the choir first as gospeller in November 1731 and then as minor canon in December 1732. He was presented to the Norwich parishes of St Martin at Palace and St John Timberhill, and was vicar of Calthorpe and Thwaite 1734-39. Three times he preached the Good Friday sermon at the cathedral, and in 1732 he was chosen to deliver the series of Hall's Sacramental Lectures. He was granted the freedom of Norwich in 1733. In 1739 he left Norwich for Hertfordshire where he held a number of parishes until his death on 5 February 1754.
(AC; Blomefield IV and VI; Millican 2)

Joseph Reding (1635-c. 1646) graduated from King's College, Cambridge in 1623 and was ordained in 1625. He became a minor canon in January 1635 and was presented to the rectory of St Augustine's, Norwich. He was admonished in 1639 for being frequently absent from the choir. By December 1644, when choral services in the cathedral had ceased, the chapter noted that he had been absent from Norwich for six months and consequently his salary was paid to his wife. In 1646 St Augustine's was sequestered and Reding was deprived of his living 'for

betaking himself to royal forces'. His salary as a minor canon was paid for that year, but there are no further references and he did not re-join the choir in 1660.
(AC; Blomefield IV; DCN 10/2/1; Matthews; W & C-H)

Thomas Sadlington (1605-1638) graduated from Corpus Christi College, Cambridge in 1602. He was appointed gospeller in September 1605 and minor canon probably in 1607. In 1606 he was admonished for striking Arthur Jackson, the epistoler, and for calling him and the rest of the choir rogues and rascals. He was vicar of Horsey 1609-15, and rector of Norwich St Peter Southgate 1623-38. He received four further admonitions for neglecting his duties, exhibiting bad manners, and for living with a woman pretending that she was his wife. His final reprimand for absence in 1630 was accompanied by an apparent expulsion from the choir, but he continued to receive his minor canon's salary until his death in 1638.
(AC; Blomefield IV; Cornall; W & C-H)

George Saunders (1608-1654) was admitted to the cathedral choir in 1608, initially as gospeller and then as minor canon. He was precentor several times between 1620 and 1643, and was master of the choristers 1621-29. He took a 21-year lease of the parsonage of Norwich St Peter Parmentergate from the dean and chapter in 1613. He was curate of St Mary in the Marsh from 1617, and vicar of Bawburgh from 1641. In February 1642 he was admonished to be more sober. He was still receiving his salary in 1646, and in 1649 was living at the house assigned to him in the precincts known as 'Greeves', though his position as a minor canon had been abolished by parliament. He died in 1654.
(Blomefield II and IV; Cornall; DCN 10/2/1; Mann Ms. 432; Metters; W & C-H)

William Scott (1691-1706) was born at Ely and educated there and at St John's College, Cambridge. He was ordained at Norwich in 1682 and was probably rector of the Suffolk parishes of Boulge (1687) and Debach (1688). He was appointed minor canon in November 1691 and nominated to the parishes of Norwich St James and St Paul. He held these positions until his death in 1706.
(AC; Blomefield IV)

John Shaw (1679-1691) may have come from Newsham near Thirsk, Yorkshire. After attending St John's College, Cambridge he was ordained at Norwich in 1679 and simultaneously appointed minor canon. He took the additional duties of epistoler (1679-80) and gospeller (1681-85) as these positions had been left unfilled since the Restoration. He was also reader of morning prayer 1680-81. The dean and chapter nominated him to be curate at Norwich St Giles in 1680 and vicar of Catton in 1687. He was expelled from the choir and deprived of his benefices in 1691 for refusing to take the oaths of allegiance to King William, having previously taken similar oaths to James II who was still living. Overton refers to him as vicar of Carleton.

(AC; Blomefield IV; Overton)

Lynne Smear (1719-1761), from Wyverstone, Suffolk was educated at Norwich School and Trinity College, Cambridge. He was ordained priest at Norwich in 1713 and admitted to the cathedral choir in December 1719, initially as gospeller and from around 1726 as minor canon. He was precentor from 1731 until at least 1752 (probably longer) and librarian from 1759. He preached the Rogation sermon in the cathedral on three occasions and the Good Friday sermon in 1754. He was presented to the parishes of Norwich St Augustine (1720), Alderford with Attlebridge (1729), Eaton (1735) and Bawburgh (1739). He served in the choir for 42 years until his death in December 1761 at the age of 76. Mann refers to a memorial stone in the cathedral.

(AC; Blomefield II and IV; Mann Ms. 432; NM, 2 January 1762)

William Smith I (1696-1729) was the son of a baker from Ipswich. He attended Pembroke College, Cambridge and was ordained at Norwich in March 1688. He was admitted to the cathedral choir as a probationer minor canon in December 1696, obtaining a full place one year later. He was presented to the vicarages of Stoke Holy Cross (1696) and Trowse (1710). For many years he was sacrist, and he was appointed librarian in June 1728. He died on 13 January 1729 aged 65. Blomefield records a memorial in the cathedral.

(AC; Blomefield IV)

William Smith II (1739-1776) was born in Norwich, the son of the cathedral registrar and chapter clerk. He graduated from St Catherine's College, Cambridge and was ordained deacon at Norwich in March 1739 and immediately appointed gospeller in the cathedral choir. He remained in this position for the rest of his life, apparently never seeking the place of a full minor canon. He delivered the series of Hall's Sacramental Lectures in 1741 and preached the Good Friday sermon in the cathedral in 1748 and 1749. He was precentor from 1762. His parishes included St Martin at Palace (1739), Stoke Holy Cross (1754), St John Timberhil (1762) and Westhall, Suffolk (1775). He died on 10 February 1776 at the age of 60. He was the author of a number of religious works, including articles published in *The World* and *London Magazine*, which are listed in Chambers.

(AC; Blomefield IV; Chambers; Mann Ms. 431; Turner)

Charles John Smyth (1795-1824) was the son of Joseph Smyth of Sholebrook Lodge, Northamptonshire. He attended New College, Oxford where he was awarded a BA degree in 1781, followed by an MA and fellowship in 1786. He was appointed minor canon at Norwich in July 1795 and became sacrist later the same year. He was presented to a number of benefices in the Norwich diocese - St Augustine's and St Mary in the Marsh, Norwich (1795), Great Fakenham, Suffolk (1803), St John Timberhill and St Peter Parmentergate, Norwich (1807) and Catton (1811). He resigned as minor canon and sacrist in October 1824, and he died at Great Fakenham aged 66 on 8 January 1827. His possessions, which were sold after his death, included an organ with five stops and pedals, a square piano, a collection of books and music, and around 300 of his own sermons. Like his cathedral colleague Ozias Linley, Charles Smyth seems to have been a man of unusual character. T D Eaton, writing about Edward Taylor, the Gresham professor of music, described Smyth - who was Taylor's first teacher - as 'equally remarkable for his eccentricity and his musical learning'. Smyth wrote strange letters to the prime minister, Lord Liverpool, in 1823; he contrbuted an article on acoustic theory to *The Harmonicon*; and he wrote to *The Gentlman's Magazine* attacking the low salaries paid by the dean and chapter to the organist and lay clerks at Norwich. He composed an anthem, a setting of the Te Deum and Jubilate, some hymn-tune harmonizations and two glees along with a published collection of *Chants Single and Double with a Sanctus*. The Te Deum, the voice parts of which occur in the old choirbooks at the cathedral, was performed at the annual hospital charity service held in the cathedral in July 1818. He also published *Six Letters on Singing from a Father to his Son* in 1817.

(AO; Eaton; G. Mag. 1812; NC, 11 October 1817 and 17 March 1827; Roast 1, 3 and 4; Turner)

Edward Smyth (1624-1661) became a minor canon on 11 October 1624 in place of John Woodson. He is probably the same person who graduated from Trinity College, Cambridge in 1609. He served as precentor and sacrist at various times, and in 1636 was appointed parish chaplain at Norwich St Martin at Palace. In the Parliamentary Survey of 1649 he had let the house assigned to him in the precincts. He received £4 in 1657 (the largest individual amount) out of a payment of £20 to the poor officers of the cathedral from the Trustees for the Maintenance of

Ministers. He resumed his position in the choir in 1660 but was only paid for half a year.

(AC; Blomefield IV; Cornall; Matthews; Metters; W & C-H)

Robert Snelling (1661-1664) was educated at Trinity College, Cambridge. In September 1661 he was ordained at Norwich and admitted to the cathedral choir as a minor canon. The following year he was appointed vicar of Earlham. He was given an admonition for showing a lack of respect towards the dean and prebendaries, and for negligent attendance. He left the choir in 1664 upon being appointed vicar of Denham, Suffolk.

(AC; Blomefield III)

John Sowter (c.1606-after 1646) was a singing man in the choir from around 1606. He was still being called a singing man (i.e. lay clerk) in 1615 when he was admonished for breaking a pump at the house in which he lived. He must have been ordained before 1620 as he was listed as gospeller at the reading of the statutes which required the gospeller to be a deacon. He became parish priest at St Peter Parmentergate in 1627 and was granted a 21-year lease there in 1642. He was still being paid as gospeller in 1646 even though choral services had ceased: he was not reappointed to the choir at the Restoration. It seems that he did not graduate to a full minor canon's place.

(Blomefield IV; Cornall; DCN 10/2/1; W & C-H)

Norwood Sparrow (1755-1779) from Newbury, Berkshire was educated at Christ Church, Oxford. His appointment as a minor canon is not recorded in the Chapter Book though it probably occurred towards the end of 1755 when he replaced Cropley Hatch who had been expelled. He preached the Good Friday sermon in the cathedral in 1773 and 1775. His parish appointments were to the rectories of Little Plumstead with Witton (1746) and Brundall (1775), and to the perpetual curacies of St Peter Parmentergate (1756) and St Gregory (1771) in Norwich and Great Plumstead (1763), all of which he was holding at the time of his death which took place at his house in the precincts on 24 January 1779.

(AO; Mann Ms. 432; Turner)

Christopher Stinnet (1661-1668) was born at Cambridge. He was educated at Perse School and Norwich School, the latter under his uncle William Stinnet. He graduated from Christ's College, Cambridge in 1645 and was appointed vicar of Easton, Norfolk in 1650. In January 1661 he was the first new minor canon to be admitted to the cathedral choir after the Interregnum. He served at various times

as precentor, sacrist and reader of morning prayer. In June 1662 he was suspended briefly for rudeness to the dean, and in 1667 he was admonished for being abusive to his colleague William Rampley. He was rector of the Norwich parishes of St Clement (1662) and St Augustine (1664). He died in 1668 and his widow received one pound from the dean and chapter towards his funeral expenses.
(AC; Blomefield IV; DCN 10/2/2; Peile)

John Stukeley (1691-1702) was one of three minor canons appointed in 1691 to replace those who were expelled as nonjurors. He was immediately presented to the joint benefice of Alderford with Attlebridge. In 1694 he was paid for copying anthems into the choir partbooks. He caused a great scandal in 1702 by persistently exposing himself to the women of the precincts from an attic window in the house occupied by Francis Folchier. In Dean Prideaux's own words, recorded in the Chapter Book, Stukeley had 'for several years past at the sight of women to have taken out his yard or privy part and to have rubbed it up and down in order unnaturally and wickedly to pollute himself and to tempt and corrupt the said women'. After taking statements from a number of people living in the precincts and holding several hearings, the dean summoned Stukeley on 22 August and expelled him from the choir. Stukeley appealed against the expulsion and was allowed fifteen days in which to refer the case to the bishop as visitor, but no referral was made. Instead Stukeley enlisted the support of the Jacobite party in Norwich which made various threats against the dean, in particular to bring him (the dean) before the Queen and Council. Such a possibility was dismissed by the Attorney General, and Stukeley's only success was a concession from the dean allowing him to remain in his house beyond the time of his expulsion.
(DCN 115/1; CSPD)

Charles Tillet (1706-1715) from Cambridge was educated at King's College School and Trinity College. He was ordained deacon at Norwich in September 1706 and became a minor canon at the same time. He served as curate at Norwich St James. In October 1707 the chapter agreed to buy him some books on theology in order that he could continue his studies. The chapter also paid the sum of £8 15s. in December 1710 'to quit him of an entanglement'. In October 1713 he was admonished by the dean for his over-familiarity with Sarah Bayly, the wife of a Norwich waggoner, and forbidden to be seen with her again. Tillet resigned from the choir in 1715. He was rector of Bittering, Norfolk from 1711 to 1730.
(AC; Blomefield IV and IX)

Thomas Tookey (1669) was ordained deacon in September 1669 and appointed minor canon at Norwich Cathedral the following month, but no payments were ever made to him and it appears that he did not take up the appointment.
(AC)

Laurence Townley (1638-1642) graduated from Trinity College, Oxford and was ordained at Norwich in September 1626. He was appointed to the Norwich parishes of St Etheldreda (1627-36) and St Edward and St Julian (1634-42). He was admitted minor canon on 4 November 1638 in place of Thomas Sadlington and was sacrist 1639/40 and precentor 1640/1. He died on 24 May 1642 though his salary continued to appear in the accounts until 1646. He was buried in the cathedral and a memorial, now removed, is recorded by Blomefield.
(AO; Blomefield IV; Cornall; DCN 10/2/1; W & C-H. Note: W & C-H give three references to 'Tho' Townley as a minor canon. In the original Chapter Book 'Tho' is twice crossed through in a contemporary hand, indicating that it was a mistake for Laurence Townley.)

John Walker (1776-1807) was born at Oxford in 1754. He became a chorister at Magdalen College in 1761 and graduated there in 1775. He was sworn in as gospeller at Norwich Cathedral in December 1776 and he remained in this position throughout his time in the choir. He was reader of morning prayer 1776-78, and he preached the Good Friday sermon in the cathedral on three occasions. He possessed a fine tenor voice which was described as 'silvery' in tone. He was presented to the perpetual curacies of Norwich St Peter Parmentergate and St John Timberhill, and was vicar of Stoke Holy Cross and Bawdsey, Suffolk, holding all the livings until his death. A collection of his *Poems* was published posthumously by his son. Three items from the collection, and one other poem by Walker, were set to music by John 'Christmas' Beckwith. Walker died on 12 November 1807 aged 53, and a memorial slab was placed in the cathedral apse. A tale concerning John Walker occurs in The Patterson Papers at Norfolk Record Office. On the night of his marriage to Hannah Fortye in October 1778 two men called at his house and forced him out into a post-chaise. They took him a few miles beyond Wymondham where they tied him up and left him some distance from a road on a quaggy common. Covered with dirt he managed to reach a cottage where he paid a poor man half a guinea to walk to Wymondham and take a horse to Norwich with news of his fate, whereupon his bride and his fellow minor canon Charles Millard (who had conducted the marriage) hired a chaise and fetched him home.
(AO; Chambers; Mann Ms. 432; NRO Patterson AC 15.4.66. Box 3 bundle 11; Turner)

Paul Whittingham (1779-1831) was born at Holywell, Oxford in January 1754. He

48

matriculated at Oriel College in 1771 and graduated there in 1774. From 1777 to 1779 he was chaplain at Magdalen College. In June 1779 he was admitted minor canon at Norwich in place of Norwood Sparrow and was given the additional duty of reader of morning prayer which he performed until 1796. His voice was described as a 'sweet alto'. He was appointed to three Norwich parishes in 1779 (St Gregory, St Peter Parmentergate and St Martin at Palace) and three others in 1781 (Arminghall, Great Plumstead and Westhall, Suffolk). In 1782 he resigned as minor canon and became epistoler, a position he held for the rest of his time in the choir. He was given the curacy of Norwich St Saviour in 1785 and then the more lucrative parishes of Martham in 1792 and Sedgeford in 1808. At the cathedral he delivered the Good Friday sermon on four occasions and preached on Christmas Day in 1815. He resigned as epistoler in April 1831 upon being appointed vicar of Badingham, Suffolk, having served in the choir for close on 52 years. He died at his house in the precincts on 14 June 1834 at the age of 80. A single chant by Paul Whittingham is included in Beckwith's collection of chants published in 1808.
(AO; Bloxam; Mann Ms. 432; Turner)

James Willins (1758-1795) was the son of a Norwich weaver, and was educated at Norwich School and Caius College, Cambridge. He was ordained priest at Norwich and appointed minor canon in 1758. He was vicar of Catton (1759) and Bawburgh (1763), and perpetual curate of St Mary in the Marsh (1771). He delivered the Good Friday sermon in 1774 and 1776. In June 1776 he became sacrist, a position he held until his death on 3 July 1795. His son of the same name was also a priest with parishes in the diocese.
(AC; G. Mag. 1795; Turner)

John Woodson (c.1618-1624) was a graduate of King's College, Cambridge. He was ordained in 1618 and became a minor canon at Norwich about this time. He was sacrist in 1621/2, and parish chaplain at St Martin at Palace from 1618 to 1636. He left the choir in 1624 and returned to King's College.
(AC; Cornall; W & C-H)

The Lay Clerks

Charles Alden (1673-1692) was admitted to the choir in December 1673. In 1680, when he was described as a 'vintner at the sign of the Charing Cross', he caused a disturbance at a meeting of Quakers in Norwich, calling them 'sons and daughters of whores'. He was admonished by the dean in 1688, together with three other lay clerks, for refusing to receive alms for the poor at the cathedral doors on Easter Day. He remained in the choir until his death on 4 August 1692.

(Blomefield IV; Tract 'Due Order of Law and Justice', 1680)

Isaac Alexander (1803-1809) was a cathedral chorister from July 1796. He was dismissed at Christmas 1803 when his voice broke but he immediately became a supernumerary lay clerk. Unusually his initial annual salary of £15 was paid from the lay clerk's fund, an account which had been created from money saved through vacancies in the choir. He continued to be paid in this manner until Michaelmas 1808 when he was admitted to a full lay clerk's place. In December 1808 he was one of the signatories to a successful petition by the lay clerks for an increase in pay. He resigned from the choir in July 1809. He had a composition published around 1807 which was entitled *When day has smil'd a soft farewell*. It was described as 'A favorite Glee as sung at the Hall Concerts, Norwich'.

(DCN 33/21 and 24; DCN 39/49 and 52)

William Alsey - see Minor Canons

Nicholas Bagley (1663) was appointed lay clerk in May 1663 and assigned a house in the precincts, but he seems to have spent only a few months in the choir for which he was paid the sum of three pounds.

Anthony Beck - see Minor Canons

Cuthbert Beckley (1663-1665) joined the choir as a lay clerk in 1663 and was formally admitted in January 1664 and assigned a house in the precincts. In August 1664 he was admonished for poor attendance, and he left the choir in 1665.

Edward Beckwith (1751-1793). The youngest son of John Beckwith I, Edward Beckwith was born on 2 June 1734. He was admitted to the cathedral choir as a lay clerk in October 1751 at the age of seventeen. In November 1759 he became master of the choristers. By this time he was established as a music teacher

in the city, and when the young James Hook left Norwich for London in 1763 Beckwith solicited for Hook's pupils, claiming that he was 'sub-organist' at the cathedral. In January 1769 he was elected organist at St Peter Mancroft in place of the blind Samuel Cooke who was considered to be unequal to the duties, but Beckwith allowed Cooke to retain his position and salary, and acted as his deputy until Cooke's death in 1780. Throughout the 1770s Beckwith put on an annual benefit concert comprising vocal and instrumental music mainly taken from the works of Handel. At the cathedral he became the main music copyist, and between 1760 and 1791 he was paid for writing 1750 sheets of music (i.e. 3500 pages) into the choir partbooks. In February 1784 he was admonished by the dean and chapter for neglecting his duties both as a lay clerk and as master of the choristers. Rather than dismissing him, the dean invited Beckwith's son, John 'Christmas' Beckwith, to return to Norwich from Oxford where he had been trained, to act as his father's assistant. This resulted in a division of duties: Edward, as master of the choristers, was concerned with giving the boys a basic education, while John, as assistant master, was responsible for their musical training. Along with his other duties, Edward Beckwith maintained his position as a lay clerk until his death on 30 December 1793, serving in all for 42 years. He was known as 'Ned'.
(Mann Ms. 430; Newman)

Henry Beckwith (1729-1730) was born in 1702, the younger brother of John Beckwith I. His time in the choir was very short. He became a lay clerk in December 1729 but was deceased by April 1730 when his place was taken by Thomas Gibbon. He was a worsted weaver and had been granted the freedom of Norwich in 1728.
(Mann Ms. 430; Millican 2; Roast 2)

John Beckwith I (1719-1750). This was the first member of the Beckwith family to sing in the cathedral choir. He was admitted as a lay clerk in May 1719 at the age of eighteen, having been granted two hours off each day during his apprenticeship to William Russell, a worsted weaver, so that he could attend the cathedral. He became a freeman of Norwich in 1722. Blomefield noted that he was master of the choristers in 1745, though it is likely that he was appointed long before that date, possibly as early as 1729 when James Finch died. He received payment for copying music into the cathedral choirbooks in 1735, 1739-41 and 1749, and there are examples of his work in manuscripts 7 and 10 at the cathedral library. He

died on 12 December 1750 aged 50, and was buried in the cathedral.
(Blomefield IV; Mann Ms. 430; Millican 2; Roast 2 and 4)

John Beckwith II (1746-1800). Second son of John Beckwith I and brother of Edward, this member of the family was initially known as John Beckwith 'junior' to distinguish him from his father, but later as 'senior' to avoid confusion with his nephew John 'Christmas' Beckwith. A memorial slab in the cathedral cloisters records that he had served the cathedral for 64 years at the time of his death in 1800, indicating that he was probably a chorister from around 1736. He became a lay clerk in 1746 and held this position for the rest of his life. For a few years in the 1750s he copied music into the cathedral choirbooks and was master of the choristers until both jobs were taken over by Edward Beckwith. Outside the cathedral he pursued a trade as a glover and breeches maker until, in 1771, he publicly announced that he was quitting his business to open a school in the lower close. The venture was obviously successful: within five years he gave notice that he was unable to accept any more pupils. After his death his widow continued to run the school in partnership with William Sayer who had been her husband's assistant. Beckwith was a capable composer, writing some thirty anthems and five service settings which were well regarded in their day. In June 1775 he was given ten guineas by the dean and chapter 'as an acknowledgement of his care and skill in furnishing music for the choir'. Some of the music, which is Handelian in character, can be found in the old cathedral manuscript books but much of it has been lost and not a single piece survives in complete form. Beckwith died aged 72 on 18 May 1800 having served as a lay clerk for 53 years.
(Mann Ms. 430; Roast 1 and 4)

John 'Christmas' Beckwith (1785-1803) was the most talented member of the Beckwith family and one of Norwich's finest musicians. He was the eldest son of Edward Beckwith, the lay clerk and master of the cathedral choristers, and was born on 25 December 1759. He was sent to Oxford for his musical training and was initially apprenticed to William Hayes at Magdalen College. When William Hayes died he assisted Philip Hayes at New College. On 1 June 1784 the dean and chapter at Norwich, dissatisfied with Edward Beckwith's work with the choristers, invited John Beckwith to return to Norwich to act as his father's deputy. In fact, an entirely new job was created for him: his father remained as master of the boys with responsibility for their education, whilst John was the assistant master of the boys responsible for their musical training. The new post attracted a salary of £30 a year, compared to the eight pounds paid to the master of the boys, reflecting no doubt the chapter's determination to appoint a person of sufficient calibre to improve the state of music at the cathedral. John Beckwith took up the job at Midsummer 1784. In June 1785 he became supernumerary lay clerk, gaining a full place in December of the same year and being assigned a house in the precincts. He became involved in almost every aspect of musical life in the city and beyond. He was joint director of three grand musical festivals held in Norwich in 1788, 1790 and 1802, and he performed at scores of other concerts of vocal and instrumental music. He took over the musical element of the annual charity service held at the cathedral for the benefit of the Norfolk and Norwich Hospital, and under his direction it became a hugely popular sacred concert performed to a crowded church and lasting three hours. He inaugurated a number of new organs in the area including those at Cromer and Wymondham. In January 1794 he became organist at the church of St Peter Mancroft, replacing his father who had died a month earlier. In 1803 he was awarded the degrees of bachelor and doctor of music by the University of Oxford. In August of that year he resigned his position as lay clerk at the cathedral. When Beckwith returned to Norwich in 1784 he probably assumed that the job of cathedral organist would become available within a reasonable time, the incumbent organist Thomas Garland having already held the post for 35 years. As it turned out Garland continued for another 24 years and Beckwith eventually succeeded to the position in 1808. He was cathedral organist for little more than a year. On 3 June 1809 he died from a paralytic stroke at the age of 49. His compositions, many of them published, included around nineteen anthems, a harpsichord sonata, an organ concerto, six voluntaries for the organ, a collection of chants, and some songs and glees.

(Mann Ms. 430; Roast 1, 2 and 3)

Thomas Beckwith (1750-1795) was the eldest son of John Beckwith I and brother of John II and Edward. He was born around 1725 and was appointed to the cathedral choir in 1750 in place of his father. The Audit Book shows that he received the enhanced salary paid to the epistoler for the year 1776, making him the last layman to hold this position. He was a barber and peruke maker with premises in Tombland, and was for many years parish clerk at St George Tombland. He died in July 1795 at the age of 70.

(Mann Ms. 430)

George Bishop (1756-1791). No record of Bishop's appointment occurs in the

Chapter Book but his first salary as a lay clerk was paid in 1756 when he replaced Thomas Hill. He was assigned a house in the precincts in 1772 and he remained in the choir until his death in June 1791. The dean and chapter gave five guineas during his last illness and for his widow after his death.
(Mann Ms. 430)

Anthony Blagrave (1665-1719) was admitted to the choir in January 1665. Between 1667 and 1691 he was paid several times for copying music into the choirbooks. He became epistoler in July 1706 and held this position until his death in January 1719. He served the cathedral for a total of 54 years. His sons Richard and John also sang in the choir.
(Mann Ms. 430)

Richard Blagrave (1683-1708), son of the foregoing Anthony Blagrave, was baptized on 25 February 1667. He seems to have joined the choir in 1683 though he was not formally admitted as a lay clerk until 1687. He was admonished in 1688, with three other lay clerks, for refusing to receive alms for the poor at the cathedral doors on Easter Day. In 1692 he took over the job of copying music into the choirbooks from his father. In 1702 he lost his voice and John Pleasants was appointed as his deputy. The diaries of Dean Prideaux make it clear that Blagrave's voice had been 'spoiled by the pox'. Pleasants received the salary of eight pounds which would normally have been paid to Blagrave, but Blagrave was allowed to retain the other earnings from his office of lay clerk. In 1706 he was paid by the dean and chapter for copying out the Parliamentary Survey. His voice apparently never returned: when John Pleasants became a full lay clerk in 1704, Joseph Finch took over as Blagrave's deputy. Blagrave died in March 1708 and by his will he left three pounds to his brother John to provide him with a new gown. Mann records a memorial slab at the west end of the cathedral. Richard Blagrave is particularly noted for having compiled the cathedral's first known anthem wordbook. In 1690 he copied out 39 anthem texts with composers' names added under the title *Cantica Sacra, or Divine Anthems usually sung in the Cathedral Church of Norwich*. It provides an important guide to the music being sung by the choir at the time. Three of the anthems are by Blagrave himself, but his music is totally lost.
(Browne; DCN 115/2; Mann Ms. 430; Oxford, Bodleian Library, Tanner Ms. 401; Roast 1)

Samuel Blyth (1795-1837) was a plasterer and for many years he was engaged by the dean and chapter to carry out work to the cathedral and to their properties in the precincts. In August 1795 he was appointed lay clerk following the death of

Thomas Beckwith. He was a popular soloist, singing a Handel aria at the hospital charity service in the cathedral in 1796 and then, in the next two years, appearing at not less than eight local concerts whose chief promoters were Michael Sharp and John Beckwith. In 1833 he was appointed surveyor to the Norwich Paving Commissioners. He died on 15 December 1837 aged 67 having been a lay clerk for 42 years.

(Mann Ms. 430; NM, various 1796-99)

Charles Bramhall (1665-1682) was admitted to the choir as a lay clerk in January 1665. He was paid for 'setting the psalms' (1665-82) and for 'naming the anthems' (1681-82). He was admonished by the dean in 1667 'to use more diligence and procure more knowledge to himself in the art of music ... he having been formerly admitted upon his promise to fit himself for the said place which he said was only for want of practice'. He died in 1682.

Richard Browne (1791-1841) came from Worcester and was a chorister at Magdalen College, Oxford where he matriculated in 1778 at the age of seventeen. He was formally admitted alto lay clerk at Norwich in July 1791 and became master of the choristers in 1794 following the death of Edward Beckwith. He was awarded a higher salary than Beckwith 'in consideration of his teaching the boys arithmetic as well as reading and writing'. How long he was schoolmaster is not clear, though it was probably until 1808 when (for reasons unknown) he was absent from the choir until October 1809, and the boys were being taught by William Sayer. He resigned his office in June 1841 upon completing fifty years in the choir and was awarded a pension of £40 a year. He died on 17 August 1843 aged 83.

(AO; Mann Ms. 430)

Timothy Browne (1689-1711) was a worsted weaver by trade. He became a lay clerk in 1689, replacing James Cooper who had been appointed organist, though he was only formally admitted to the choir in August 1690. He received £2 10s. for copying music into the choirbooks in 1695. In March 1711 he advertised that he was teaching children to read at his rooms in the precincts. He died on 21 June 1711 aged 49.

(Blomefield IV; Mann Ms. 430; NG, 17 March 1711)

Robert Burgess (1738-1757). There are no entries in the Chapter Book recording the appointment of this singer, but he was first paid as a lay clerk in 1738 when he

replaced Samuel Cooke who had resigned on 31 December 1737. Burgess was in the choir for twenty years until his death on 3 December 1757 at the age of 60.
(Mann Ms. 430)

John Carlton (1603-1626) was a singing man from 1603 and epistoler from 1606 until his death in 1626. In 1614 he abused Thomas Askew, minor canon and master of the choristers, calling him 'ass, fool and dunce'. He was suspended by the chapter but reinstated after making an apology. Someone of the same name applied for a clerk's place at Eton College in 1617.
(Cornall; W & C-H)

Martin Carlton (1614-1671) was a singing man from 1614 until the Interregnum and again after the Restoration. He was admonished in 1644 for disrespect 'in words and gestures' towards the dean. At the time of the Parliamentary Survey in 1649 he was still living in the house assigned to him at the south end of the cloisters, even though his position in the choir had been abolished. He received £2 10s. in 1657 out of a payment of £20 to the poor officers of the cathedral from the Trustees for the Maintenance of Ministers. He resumed his place in the choir in 1660 which he retained until his death in December 1671.
(Cornall; Mann Ms. 431; Matthews; Metters; W & C-H)

Redmaine Carlton (1616-1665), probably brother of the foregoing, was baptized at St George Tombland on 8 May 1593. He was a singing man in the choir from 1616 until the Interregnum and again after the Restoration. In some years he was required to begin the psalms for which he received an additional payment. He repaired the cathedral clock in 1638/9. In the 1649 Parliamentary Survey he had let the house assigned to him against the north wall of the cathedral, which he shared with Anthony Beck, to various poor people at an annual rent of £4. He received £2 10s. in 1657 out of a payment of £20 to the poor officers of the cathedral from the Trustees for the Maintenance of Ministers. He resumed his place in the choir in 1660 and was again responsible for beginning the psalms. He was buried on 19 January 1665.
(Cornall; Mann Ms. 431; Matthews; Metters; W & C-H)

William Clabburn (1781-1785) was engaged as a supernumerary lay clerk in December 1781, attaining a full place in the choir in April 1785. By then he had become a popular local soloist with appearances at several concerts at Quantrill's Gardens in 1784 and 1785. He also sang at a concert to mark the opening of a new

organ by John Beckwith at Halesworth on 17 June 1785. His promising career ended with his unexpectedly early death at the age of 23 on 24 June 1785. The day before his death he had taken his usual place in the cathedral choir.
(Mann Ms. 431; NM, 2 July 1785)

John Clarke (1758-1770). Little is known about this lay clerk except that he replaced Robert Burgess in 1758 and remained in the choir until his death on 20 March 1770.
(NM, 24 March 1770)

William Cobbold (1611-1639) was born in Norwich in 1560, the son of a goldsmith. He was paid for singing in the cathedral choir in 1581/2, and in 1594 he was granted a patent as organist to commence at Ladyday 1595. He seems to have occupied the post until William Inglott, who had been organist until 1591, resumed his former position in 1611. Cobbold stood down and became a lay clerk, although he probably continued to share some of the organ duties with Inglott. He was still singing in the choir in 1638 at the age of 78. He died the following year and despite his own wish to be buried in the cathedral, he was interred in the south aisle of Beccles parish church alongside his first wife and son. An inscription to his memory remains there. Cobbold was a man of substance: he inherited property in Norwich from his father which he sold in 1635 for £320. Under his will he left money for the singing men and choristers of the cathedral choir and the two organ blowers, as well as for the poor people of the precincts and the parishes of St Andrew, St John Timberhill and St George Tombland. He was also a competent composer: Thomas Morley included his madrigal *With wreathes of rose and laurel* in the collection *The Triumphes of Oriana* (1601), and eleven of his psalm tunes were published in Thomas Este's *The Whole Book of Psalms* (1592). He also composed a substantial anthem *In Bethlehem town* and a number of consort pieces for voices and viols.
(Cornall; DCN 10/2/1; Roast 1; Shaw; W & C-H)

Edward Cooke (1670-1704) became a lay clerk in July 1670. From 1691 onwards he received an extra five shillings each year for 'naming the anthem'. He died on 11 June 1704 at the age of 68, having spent 34 years in the choir.
(Blomefield IV)

Samuel Cooke (1729-1737 and 1741-1746) appears to have spent two periods in the choir. His first admission as a lay clerk occurred in April 1729 but he resigned his position on 31 December 1737. During 1740 he reappeared in the choir sharing singing duties with John Hewitt, and when Hewitt resigned in May 1741 Cooke was reappointed in his place. His second term ended in 1746 when he was replaced by John Beckwith II.

William Cooke (1756-1800) was first paid as a lay clerk in 1756. In 1772 he was assigned a property in the precincts called Coates Tenement. Between the years of 1769 and 1781 he shared with Edward Beckwith the job of copying music into the choirbooks, earning more than £32 for his labours. In the 1780 Poll his occupation is shown as schoolmaster. He died on 10 February 1800.
(NC, 15 February 1800)

James Cooper (1679-1689). For the year to Michaelmas 1680 Cooper was paid for officiating as a probationary lay clerk. In November 1680 he was admitted to a full lay clerk's position on the death of Braithwaite Sowter and was assigned Sowter's house in the precincts. He seems to have made a satisfactory impression on the dean and chapter who awarded him a gratuity of £5 in 1685 'for his good service to the church'. In September 1689 he was appointed organist and master of the choristers in place of Thomas Pleasants, and he remained as organist until his death in January 1721. An inscribed memorial is in the floor of the cathedral. When the cathedral organ was repaired by Christian Smith in 1699, Cooper apparently paid for a trumpet stop to be added. Cooper was a prolific, though undistinguished, composer. At least 26 anthems, three services, a setting of the funeral sentences, and fourteen chants can be identified in manuscript books which have a Norwich Cathedral provenance.
(Boston; Mann Ms. 431; Roast 1 and 4)

John Cox (1811-1855) was a cathedral chorister from 1799 to 1805. He was readmitted to the choir as an alto lay clerk in October 1811, and was master of the choristers from around 1819 until 1830. In April 1818 he sang a solo from an anthem by Maurice Greene which prompted a visitor to the cathedral to write to a local newspaper describing his voice as 'sweet, rich and brilliant'. With James Cupper and two choristers he sang an anthem at the funeral of John Charles Beckwith, the cathedral organist, which was held at St Peter Mancroft in October 1819. He was a soloist at several of the annual hospital charity services which were held at the cathedral until their demise in 1823. He was an upholsterer by trade and from 1812 he supplied the cathedral with curtains, carpets, tapestries and cushions until 1844 when he was declared bankrupt. He sang in the chorus at the

first three Triennial Festivals in 1824, 1827 and 1830. By 1854 his attendance in the cathedral choir had become very irregular and his last appearance was in March 1855. He died on 9 November 1855 aged 67. A memorial to his long service is in the cathedral cloisters. Three of his children were musicians: William and Ellen were teachers and James Valentine was a lay clerk in the cathedral choir for fifty years.
(DCN 39/49; Mann Ms. 431; NC, 25 April 1818 and 10 November 1855)

Charles Crosley (1682-1688) was paid a full lay clerk's salary for the year to Michaelmas 1683 although his position was not confirmed by the chapter until September 1687. In that year he received an additional 2s.6d. for 'setting the psalms and naming the anthems'. His last year of service was 1688.

James Cupper (1813-1867) was a cathedral chorister from July 1796 to Christmas 1799. In 1813 he officiated in the choir as a substitute during Joseph Parnell's illness, and was admitted to a lay clerk's place upon Parnell's death in November 1813. He took a solo at the funeral service for John Charles Beckwith, the cathedral organist, held at St Peter Mancroft in October 1819. He was a member of the chorus at the Triennial Festivals from their inauguration in 1824 until 1863 (though his name is missing in 1842). When he died on 11 April 1867 at the age of 83 he had been a lay clerk for 54 years. Cupper had several business interests. He was principally a bookseller, bookbinder and stationer with premises in Rampant Horse Street, and each year from 1812 he bound and repaired books and music for the cathedral. He operated a circulating library from his bookshop. He was also a coal merchant and supplied the dean and chapter with coal for the boys' school, the vestry, and the poor of the precincts. Between 1841 and 1844 he was road surveyor for the parish of St Stephen.
(DCN 39/49; NC, 13 April 1867; NRO, PD 484/114)

Hillary Dallison (1664-1686) was admitted to the choir as a probationer at Michaelmas 1664 and granted a full lay clerk's place a year later. In 1667 he was the recipient of a payment of Royal Ayde. From 1682 to 1686 he was paid an extra five shillings a year for 'setting the psalms and naming the anthems'. His last salary was paid in 1686.

William Fenn (1816-1854) was born in Norwich in the parish of All Saints. He was admitted to the cathedral choir as an alto lay clerk in August 1816 and was a popular soloist, performing at the hospital charity services held in the cathedral in 1818, 1819, 1821 and 1823. He also sang at the funeral of Dean Turner in 1828, and at a service on the day of King William's funeral in 1837. He was master of the choristers from 1831 to 1851. He sang in the chorus at six successive Triennial Festivals between 1824 and 1839. In 1847 the cathedral organist, Zechariah Buck, wanted to appoint Thomas Harcourt in place of Fenn whose voice (he said) was putting 'everything out of tune', but Fenn would not resign. In the Census of 1851 he is shown as age 59 and a clerk at the savings bank. At a special chapter meeting held on 27 January 1854 he was allowed to retire from his office of lay clerk and was granted 'twenty five pounds per annum during the life of Mr. Hart whom he succeeds as senior clerk in the savings bank'. His place in the choir was temporarily taken by James Ling who was engaged as a supernumerary. On 5 April 1854 Fenn was given a tea service by the precentor in recognition of his 38 years in the choir. His formal resignation only came in November 1855, whereupon Ling was given a full place. Fenn was organist to the Provincial Grand Lodge of Freemasons. He died in 1857.

(DCN 120/2S/1-7; GRO; Memorandum Book 1839)

Joseph Finch (1704-1729). When lay clerk Richard Blagrave lost his voice in 1702, John Pleasants was appointed as his deputy. Pleasants was admitted to a full lay clerk's place in June 1704 and Joseph Finch took over as Blagrave's deputy. He was awarded Blagrave's annual salary of £8 but he petitioned the chapter for an increase to cover the damage to his business caused by his daily attendance at the cathedral, and was granted an additional £4 out of Blagrave's corn money. Blagrave died in March 1708 and Finch was appointed a full lay clerk in his place. He seems to have been a mercer by trade as he was paid every year by the chapter for making the choirboys' gowns. In February 1721 he became master of the boys following the death of James Cooper. Between 1721 and 1727 he was paid for copying 921 pages of music into the cathedral choirbooks: some of his work can be clearly seen in manuscript 2 in the cathedral library. He died in 1729.

(Roast 4)

Thomas Gibbon (1730-1764) was admitted to the choir in April 1730 in place of Henry Beckwith, and he occupied a position as lay clerk until his death in April 1764. No other information on this singer has come to light.

(Mann Ms. 431)

William Hall (1771-1781). Little is known about this musician beyond the payments in the Audit Book which show that he was a supernumerary lay clerk from 1771, attained a full place in 1776, and received his last salary in 1781.

Lawrence Harman (c. 1638-after 1649) first appears as a lay clerk in 1638 although his appointment, and the assignment of his house, was not recorded in the Chapter Book until December 1645. He was still being paid in 1646 even though choral services had ceased, and he was resident in his house at the time of the Parliamentary Survey in 1649, but there are no further references to him during the Interregnum and he was not reappointed to the choir in 1660.
(DCN 10/2/1; Metters; W & C-H)

Samuel Harper (1764-1785) joined the choir in 1764 following the death of Thomas Gibbon, though his place as a lay clerk was not confirmed until April 1765. He was assigned a house in the precincts called Allen's House in 1772 and he remained in the choir until his death on 24 April 1785.
(Mann Ms. 431)

John Harris (1634-1648) was formally admitted as a lay clerk on 15 March 1634. In 1638 he was paid an extra 20s. as sacrist. He was still receiving his full salary in 1646 but was deceased by May 1648 when his will was proven and his house was assigned to Anthony Beck.
(DCN 10/2/1; Mann Ms. 431; W & C-H)

John Haund (before 1620-c.1634) was already a singing man at the time the statutes were introduced in the cathedral on 5 September 1620, and he remained in that position until no later than 1634. In some years he acted as beginner of the psalms, and was paid several times for mending the cathedral clock.
(Cornall; W & C-H)

Samuel Hayden (1794-1827) was the senior member of a Norwich musical family. He was born on 20 December 1764, the eldest of eight children. Three of his brothers were musicians: Henry (born 1773) was a pupil of John 'Christmas' Beckwith and became organist at St Asaph cathedral; Thomas (born 1775) and Benjamin (born 1778) were both cathedral choristers. Samuel became a lay clerk in 1794 in the place of Edward Beckwith, and in the same year he was chosen as parish clerk of St Mary Coslany. He occupied both positions for 33 years until his death on 17 December 1827 which occurred shortly before his 63rd birthday. His son William was also a lay clerk and succeeded his father as parish clerk at St Mary Coslany.
(A. Homes, *The Hayden Musicians*, published privately (2006))

John Hewett (1737-1741) became a lay clerk in March 1737. In 1740 he seems to have shared his singing duties with Samuel Cooke, and when he resigned in 1741 Cooke took his place in the choir.

Thomas Hill (1727-1756) was a Norwich carpenter who became a lay clerk in November 1727. He was granted the freedom of Norwich in 1739. He served in the choir for 28 years and when he died on 11 February 1756 at the age of 49 he was buried in the south transept of the cathedral. A memorial slab records that he was carpenter to the cathedral for eighteen years.
(Mann Ms. 431; Millican 2)

Augustine Holl (1776-1780) was a gardener. He became a freeman of Norwich in 1752 as the son of Thomas Holl, a worsted weaver. He was appointed a supernumerary lay clerk in June 1776 at a stipend of ten pounds a year and he sang in this capacity until 1780: he was never made a full lay clerk. He voted at the 1794 Poll in the parish of St Peter Parmentergate.
(Millican 2)

Richard Hosier (1626) was admitted as a singing man in January 1626 but remained only briefly in the choir. A single payment of two pounds 'to one Hosier, a singing man' in 1663 suggests that he may have been called upon to help rebuild the choir in the early years of the Restoration.
(Cornall; W & C-H)

John Hutchinson (1689-1733) was one of the city waits for twenty years until he was dismissed in November 1698 for rudeness towards the mayor. He became a lay clerk in 1689. The chapter paid him two pounds in 1697 'for relief being grieved with sickness', and he received £1 1s. in 1720 for copying service music into the choirbooks. According to Mann he was a music master and lived in the lower close. In June 1730 he became epistoler in place of Francis Knights. He seems to have come upon hard times: three benefit concerts were given on his behalf in 1728, 1730 and 1731, and the chapter awarded him three shillings a week from a discretionary fund in December 1732 'until the next General Chapter if he lives so long'. He died in April 1733, having been in the choir for 44 years.
(Mann Ms. 431; NG, 27 April 1728, 4 April 1730 and 14 August 1731; Stephen)

John Jackson (1669-1672) came to Norwich following a brief period as instructor in music at Ely Cathedral. He was appointed lay clerk in December 1669 and

simultaneously became master of the choristers in succession to Richard Ayleward. The following May he gave a bond to the cathedral authorities that he would fulfil his duties as a lay clerk for a period of three years. In June 1670 the dean paid £7 15s. 'to relieve John Jackson out of prison': the reason for his incarceration is not specified, although it was probably for debt. He failed to honour his bond and left the choir in 1672 with Thomas Pleasants taking his place as master of the choristers. He seems to have spent some time in London as vicar choral at St Paul's Cathedral, and then in September 1674 he became organist and vicar choral at Wells Cathedral where he remained until his death in 1688. He was a prolific and versatile composer, writing twelve anthems, three service settings, three devotional pieces, two compositions to Latin texts, four chants to the Venite, and a setting of the Burial Service. In addition seven catches, three songs and a keyboard piece were published in various contemporary collections.
(Oxford, Bodleian Library, Tanner Ms. 133; Roast 1)

John Keymer (1733-1736). This lay clerk was admitted to the choir in December 1733 and resigned his place in June 1736.

Francis Knights (1686-1730) began singing in the choir in 1686 when he replaced Thomas Mowting who had died on 3 February, but his formal admission as a lay clerk occurred in September 1687. In April 1688 he was admonished, along with three other lay clerks, for ignoring an order by the dean to receive alms for the poor at the cathedral doors on Easter Sunday. He received a second admonition for threatening to beat the verger who delivered the order to him. Thereafter, he seems to have amended his ways. In 1721 he received forty shillings from the chapter as a gift 'in his present necessity'. He also received payment in 1726 for cleaning and repairing the altar and tapestry cloths. He resigned his position as lay clerk in 1729 to replace John Smith as epistoler (at an enhanced salary) and was assigned Smith's house. The preferment lasted only a few months: he died in 1730 after serving in the choir for 44 years.
(DCN 12/59)

Alexander Leak (1786-1793) was a supernumerary lay clerk between 1786 and 1793. He was apparently never granted a full place in the choir, though he was awarded a benefaction of five guineas by the chapter in 1792.

Cornelius Manley (1717-1719) was appointed lay clerk in November 1717. On

10 January 1719 he became epistoler upon the death of Anthony Blagrave, and was assigned Blagrave's house, but he himself died the following month on 25 February at the age of 31. In spite of his short tenure a memorial was placed in the cathedral. Goodman described him (perhaps wrongly) as 'organist'.
(Blomefield IV; Goodman part 1, p.5)

Thomas Martin (1666-1683) became a lay clerk at the beginning of 1666 and was formally admitted in November that year. In the 1680s he was commissioned by the dean and chapter to undertake a survey of their estates. He appears to have left the choir in 1683, to be replaced by Richard Blagrave. He was buried on 30 June 1684.
(Atherton and Holderness; Mann Ms. 432)

Thomas Meares (1639-after 1657) was admitted to the choir as a singing man on 15 November 1639 and assigned a house in the precincts. In 1642 he was admonished for showing disrespect towards the dean and prebendaries. In the Parliamentary Survey of 1649 he had let his house to William Greenwood. He received £1 10s. in 1657 from a payment of £20 to the poor officers of the cathedral from the Trustees for the Maintenance of Ministers. He probably died during the Interregnum as he did not return to the choir in 1660 and was described as 'deceased' when his house was assigned to Samuel Norman in February 1661.
(Matthews; Metters; W & C-H)

William Monting (1729) became a lay clerk on 1 July 1729 in place of Joseph Finch, but he died sometime before 25 November that year when he was replaced by John Swanton.

Thomas Moody (1608-1636) was a singing man from 1608 until his death in 1636. He was also a city wait from around 1616. Along with two other waits he was dismissed from his job in 1622 (for harbouring vagrants) but soon reinstated and issued with two treble hautboys, a chain and a flag. In 1616 he was granted a 21-year lease by the corporation of a corner house at Suffragan's Tenements in King Street, with a stable, at a rent of 52s. per annum. He was buried on 20 July 1636.
(Cornall; Mann Ms. 432; Stephen; W & C-H)

Robert Morrant (1668-1669) was a cathedral chorister between 1664 and 1667. He became a probationer lay clerk the following year, being paid from Ladyday 1668, but he served only to Midsummer 1669.
(DCN 10/2/2; Mann Ms.432)

Samuel Morris (1770-1816) from Trowse replaced John Clarke in the choir in May 1770 though his place as a lay clerk was not confirmed until March 1772 when he was assigned a house in the precincts. In the 1784 Poll his trade was shown as worsted weaver. On three occasions he was paid for copying relatively small quantities of music into the choirbooks. Twice he received a benefaction from the chapter - five guineas in 1794 and six guineas in 1795. He died in 1816 and the chapter paid his widow an annual gratuity of five pounds until Christmas 1822.
(Mann Ms. 432)

Thomas Mowting (1633-1686) was admitted as a singing man on 27 April 1633. He was assigned a house in the precincts which he vacated in 1646 for minor canon Edward Smyth, taking instead a small house on the way to the ferry. In the Parliamentary Survey of 1649 he had let this house at a rent of £2 a year. He received £1 in 1657 (the lowest individual sum) out of a payment of £20 to the poor officers of the cathedral from the Trustees for the Maintenance of Ministers. He returned to the choir in 1660 and remained there until his death on 3 February 1686 when he was aged 82. Blomefield records a former memorial at the cathedral.
(Blomefield IV; Matthews; Metters; W & C-H)

Samuel Newman - see Minor Canons.

Samuel Norman (1660-1667) was the first new appointment to the choir after the Interregnum, being formally admitted as a lay clerk in December 1660. He received an admonition from the dean in 1665 for being absent from services. His last salary was paid at Ladyday 1667.

Joseph Parnell (1780-1813) was around 40 years of age when he became a lay clerk in the cathedral choir. He was initially admitted as a supernumerary in 1780 and obtained a full place the next year. Following the death of Edward Beckwith in 1793 Parnell became the chief copyist, receiving payment in most years for writing parts into the cathedral choirbooks. His busiest years were 1807 and 1812: in each year he copied more than one thousand pages of music. In September 1796 he was appointed clerk of St Luke's chapel at the cathedral. From 1801 he had recurring spells of illness and received financial assistance from the lay clerks' fund. A concert for his benefit was given at Chapelfield House in April 1804, being a performance of Handel's *Judas Maccabaes* conducted by John 'Christmas' Beckwith. By 1813 he needed a substitute in the choir. He died on 10 November 1813 at the

age of 74. Parnell was a capable all-round musician. He performed at many public concerts in Norfolk and Suffolk, sometimes as a vocalist and on other occasions playing violin, 'cello or double bass. He was a principal instrumentalist at a grand concert at Wymondham Abbey in 1793 to mark the opening of a new organ. A few of his compositions are known about. For the church he wrote three hymn tunes and a chant, the latter (which was adapted from music by Handel) being included in Beckwith's collection of chants published in 1808. His secular music consisted of pieces for an unnamed pantomime given at the Norwich Theatre in 1784, and some incidental music to a staged entertainment called *The Offspring of Fancy* in 1786. Unfortunately, not a note of the music seems to have survived. Parnell also operated a teaching practice, one of his pupils being the composer George Perry. Parnell's first wife died in June 1785 and later that year he married Mary Beckwith, sister of John 'Christmas' Beckwith. Several of their children were musicians: Michael was a violinist who performed at the Assembly House when he was only thirteen; John was also thirteen when he was appointed organist at St George Colegate, by which time he was already acting as sub-organist at the cathedral; Mary was of similar age when she sang two Handel arias at the hospital charity service held in the cathedral in 1808; and Robert, George and William were all cathedral choristers.
(Mann Ms. 432; Roast 1)

Benjamin Paul (1748-1775). No record of his appointment can be found but Benjamin Paul replaced John Reynolds who died in 1748. He may have become a freeman of Norwich in 1737 as the son of William Paul, a Norwich tailor. He was assigned a house in the precincts called Larwood's Tenement in 1772. He died on 19 June 1775.
(Mann Ms. 432; Millican 2)

Edward Payne (1721-1725). This was a one-off appointment of a supernumerary singing man. Payne was appointed at Christmas 1721 to attend once a day in the choir, and he occupied this position until Ladyday 1725. Although he received the same salary as the lay clerks he would not have been entitled to their additional emoluments.

John Pleasants (1702-1751) was the son of Thomas Pleasants, organist of the cathedral 1670-1689, and brother of the following. He first sang in the cathedral choir in October 1702 when he acted as deputy for lay clerk Richard Blagrave who had lost his voice. When a place in the choir became available with the death of Edward Cooke in June 1704, Pleasants was admitted as a full lay clerk. In 1713 he was publicly admonished in front of the choir for speaking rude and abusive words about the dean, as witnessed by Henry Semons, the verger, and his wife. He ran into debt and in 1716 a receiver was appointed to deal with all claims against him. He was assigned his brother's house in the precincts upon William's death in October 1717. In 1728 he was again reported for speaking rudely about the dean and was given a second admonition. In 1733 he replaced John Hutchinson as epistoler and he remained in this position until his death in August 1751. He was in the choir for just under 49 years.

(Mann Ms. 432)

William Pleasants (1692-1717), brother of the foregoing, was born in 1675. He became a lay clerk in September 1692, and in 1698 he took over from James Cooper as master of the boys. Four times between 1695 and 1708 he was paid for copying music into the cathedral choirbooks. He received an admonition in 1703 for lack of diligence in teaching the boys, and again in 1704 for leading a 'loose, disorderly and wicked life'. On the latter occasion he was made to make a public confession on his knees in the chapter house, and the job of teaching the boys was given back to Cooper. In 1707 a new organ was built at the church of St Peter Mancroft and Pleasants became the church's first organist. He held this position while retaining his place as lay clerk until his death in October 1717. Pleasants was a minor composer. Two verse anthems, a service setting, and a chant are to be found in manuscripts which have a Norwich Cathedral provenance, though they are all in some way incomplete.

(Mann Ms. 432; Roast 1)

Philip Priest (1711-1721) became a lay clerk in September 1711. He was given an allowance in lieu of a house until 1717 when he was assigned a property in the precincts formerly occupied by Joseph Finch. He was admonished in September 1721 for his poor attendance in the choir during the preceding year. He died at the age of 29 on 17 November 1721. Mann knew of an Evening Service in F composed by 'Mr Priest' in the old music books at the cathedral, but this can no longer be found.

(Blomefield IV; Mann Ms. 432)

Thomas Purton (1614-1639) was admitted as a singing man - a tenor - on 10 December 1614 and appointed to begin the psalms which were sung before and after the sermon. He became epistoler in 1626. On 3 February 1627 he was called before the dean accused of 'drawing away' the head chorister, Robert Gransborowe, without permission. He was dismissed from the choir but, on the intervention of the chorister, this was rescinded and instead he was given an admonition 'to behave himself honestly and soberly'. He died in 1639.
(Cornall; W & C-H)

Thomas Quash (c. 1612-1638) was a singing man from around 1612, or possibly earlier. He received three admonitions for absence and was threatened with a reduction in wages. He was absent from the swearing-in of the new statutes in September 1620 and took his oath a month later. He was also a city wait, being appointed on 13 June 1612. Along with two other waits he was dismissed in 1622 (for harbouring vagrants) but reinstated a week later. He became a freeman of Norwich in 1613. He was buried on 9 December 1638.
(Cornall; Mann Ms. 432; Millican 1; Stephen; W & C-H)

John Reynolds (1730-1748) was admitted to the choir in June 1730 in place of John Hutchinson who had been appointed epistoler. He kept his place as lay clerk until his death in April 1748.
(Mann Ms. 432)

Peter Sandley (c. 1606-1668), also called Sandlyn, was a singing man from around 1606, and a city wait from 1617 playing sackbut and recorder. He became a freeman of Norwich in 1622. He was admonished in 1620 for 'malpertness and sauciness' towards the dean, and again in 1639 for being under the influence of drink when he deputized at the organ for Richard Gibbs, causing 'great confusion in the choir'. Between 1615 and 1624 he was paid three times for repairing the organ. He was still receiving his choir salary in 1646 and was assigned a house in the precincts, but by 1649 - when his position in the choir had been abolished - he had let the house to Thomas Norgate for £4 a year. He received £2 10s. in 1657 out of a payment of £20 to the poor officers of the cathedral from the Trustees for the Maintenance of Ministers. He was readmitted to the choir when services resumed in 1660 and was paid for teaching the choirboys during the first year. The dean and chapter assigned his house to minor canon Christopher Stinnet in 1662 but ordered Stinnet to pay the annual rent of £4 to Sandley. He received his last salary at Michaelmas 1668, more than 60 years after his first admission to the choir.

Goodman believed that he lived to the age of 89 and was a singing man in the time of Queen Elizabeth.
(Cornall; Goodman, part 1, p. 14; Matthews; Metters; Millican I; Stephen; W & C-H)

William Sayer (1800-1842) was assistant to John Beckwith II at the boarding school which Beckwith ran in the lower close. When Beckwith died in 1800 his widow continued to run the school in partnership with Sayer. At the cathedral Sayer replaced Beckwith in the choir, being appointed lay clerk in September 1800. He was master of the choristers for several years, probably from 1808 to 1819. In the 1841 Census he was shown as being 70 years of age and living at Thorpe Terrace, but in 1844 he was assigned Bramel House in the lower close by the dean and chapter. His regular attendance in the choir appears to have ceased in 1842, though he continued to receive a basic salary, presumably as a pension. He died in 1860 by which time he must have been approaching 90 years old.
(GRO)

Roger Serret (1672-1673) was a probationer from April 1672 and became a full lay clerk in January 1673, but by December of that year his place had been taken by Charles Alden.

Francis Smith (1719-1727) was paid for singing in the choir in 1719 and formally admitted as a lay clerk in December 1720. He was assigned a house in the precincts in November 1721. He died in 1727 and was replaced by Thomas Hill.

John Smith (1706-1729) was appointed lay clerk in July 1706. The following year he was paid 10s. by the chapter for four anthems, but it is not clear what this referred to. He became epistoler in February 1719, a position he held until his resignation in December 1729.

Braithwaite Sowter (1661-1680) was probably the son of gospeller John Sowter. He was baptized on 6 August 1612 and was therefore approaching 50 years of age when he was appointed lay clerk in December 1661. Between 1667 and 1670 he was paid for copying music into the choir and organ books. He remained a lay clerk until his death on 8 November 1680 aged 68. He composed a verse anthem *O Lord God of my Salvation*, and acquired a remarkable collection of one hundred music books (mostly printed) which he bequeathed to the dean and chapter.
(Browne; Mann Ms. 432; Roast 1)

Richard Sparrow (1704-1706). After a long period when there was no epistoler or gospeller (see main text), Sparrow was appointed epistoler in October 1704 and seems to have served in that position until he was replaced by Anthony Blagrave in July 1706.

John Swanton (1729-1775) was a twisterer by trade. He became a lay clerk in November 1729 and replaced Jacob Votier as epistoler in 1756. He held this position until his death on 3 December 1775 at the age of 75, by which time he had served in the choir for 46 years. He was also clerk of St Paul's parish for 34 years.
(Mann Ms. 432)

John Taze (1675). The dean and chapter agreed to pay John Taze £10 a year as a probationer commencing from Ladyday 1675, but no payments appear to have been made. He had been a cathedral chorister in 1669 when Richard Ayleward was organist.
(DCN 10/2/2; Mann Ms. 432)

Jacob Votier (1722-1755). This lay clerk was admitted to the choir in January 1722. From 1752 he appears to have become the epistoler in place of John Pleasants with the enhanced salary appropriate to that office. His last salary was paid to Michaelmas 1755.

John Wilson (1675-1679). A note to the accounts for the year to Michaelmas 1675 records an agreement by the dean and chapter 'that in case John Wilson shall duly perform the office of lay clerk in the cathedral, he shall for his said service receive £8 per annum as probationer to be continued until a lay clerk's place fall void'. As the choir already had its full complement of eight lay clerks this was a concessionary position. Wilson sang in this capacity for four years until 1679 but no vacancy became available. A further chapter order in December 1681 authorized payment to him as a supernumerary for the year ensuing, but no payment appears to have been made. Wilson had been a cathedral chorister in the years 1667-69 under Richard Ayleward.
(DCN 10/2/2; Mann Ms. 432)

Edward Woodward (1800-1833) became a lay clerk in September 1800 following the death of William Cooke. From 1817 he was the chief music copyist in succession to Joseph Parnell. His annual bills to the dean and chapter show in detail the pieces which he wrote into the choirbooks and give the clearest indication of the choir's repertory during the 1820s. The composers listed in the 1820 account are Boyce, Camidge, Clarke-Whitfield, Farrant, Hayes, Jackson (of Exeter), Linley (the minor canon) and Nares. Woodward taught music from his house in the lower close. He died on 16 December 1833 at the age of 73. A subscription was raised for his widow to which the chapter gave ten pounds. Woodward's son, also Edward, was a music teacher with a shop and circulating library in Pottergate Street. He was a prolific composer particularly of piano music. Soon after his father's death he moved to Liverpool where he remained for the rest of his life.

(Mann Ms. 439; NC, 21 December 1833)

James Wyth (1686-1729) sang in the choir from 1686 and was formally admitted in September 1687. The following year he received an admonition, together with three other lay clerks, for disobeying the dean's order to receive alms for the poor at the cathedral doors on Easter Sunday. He received payment for copying anthems and services into the choirbooks in 1715 and 1717. He was probably the same James Wyth who, as a worsted weaver, was granted the freedom of Norwich on 22 August 1722. He died at the age of 65 on 1 May 1729 after 43 years in the choir.

(Mann Ms. 432; Millican 2)

Bibliography

Atherton I and Holderness B A	'The Dean and Chapter Estates since the Reformation', *Norwich Cathedral: Church, City and Diocese, 1096-1996* (eds. I Atherton, E Fernie, C Harper-Bill and H Smith), London (1996), pp. 665-687
Atherton I and Morgan V	'Revolution and Retrenchment: The Cathedral, 1630-1720', *Norwich Cathedral: Church, City and Diocese, 1096-1996*, London (1996), pp. 540-575
Black C	*The Linleys of Bath*, London (1911)
Blomefield F	*An Essay towards a Topographical History of the County of Norfolk*, 11 volumes, London (1805-1810)
Bloxam J R	*A Register of the Residents, Fellows, ... Choristers and other members of Saint Mary Magdalen College in the University of Oxford*, 8 volumes, Oxford (1853-1885)
Boston N	*The Musical History of Norwich Cathedral*, Norwich (1963)
Browne T	*Repertorium: or some Account of the Tombs and Monuments in the Cathedral of Norwich in 1680*, London (1712)
Bumpus J S	*A History of English Cathedral Music 1549-1889*, London (1908)
Chambers J	*A General History of the County of Norfolk intended to convey all the information of a Norfolk Tour*, Norwich (1829)
Cornall A	*The Practice of Music at Norwich Cathedral c.1558-1649*, unpublished dissertation for the degree of M Mus., University of East Anglia (1976)
Eade Sir P	*The Norfolk and Norwich Hospital 1770-1900*, London (1900)
Eaton T D	*Musical Criticism and Biography*, London (1872)
Eshleman D (ed.)	*The Committee Books of the Theatre Royal Norwich 1768-1825*, London (1970)
Fawcett T	*Music in Eighteenth-Century Norwich and Norfolk*, Norwich (1979)

Foster J   (1) *Alumni Oxonienses: the Members of the University of Oxford 1500-1714*, 4 volumes, Nendeln reprint (1968)

              (2) *Alumni Oxonienses: the Members of the University of Oxford 1715-1886*, 4 volumes, Oxford (1888)

Goodman R   *The Records of Norwich*, part I, London (1736)

Houlbrooke R   'Refoundation and Reformation, 1538-1628', *Norwich Cathedral: Church, City and Diocese, 1096-1996*, London (1996), pp.507-539

Howard J J (ed.)   *Miscellanea Genealogica et Heraldica*, London (1880)

Jewson C B   *The Baptists in Norfolk*, London (1957)

Kitton F G   *Zechariah Buck: A Centenary Memoir*, London (1899)

Le Huray P G   *Music and the Reformation in England 1549-1660*, Cambridge (1967)

Mann A H   *Norwich Cathedral Musicians:* handwritten notes in three volumes at Norfolk Record Office Mss. 430-432

Matthews A G   *Walker Revised, being a revision of John Walker's Sufferings of the Clergy during the Grand Rebellion 1642-1660*, Oxford (1948)

Metters G A (ed.)   *The Parliamentary Survey of Dean and Chapter Properties in and around Norwich in 1649*, Norfolk Record Society, volume 51 (1985)

Millican P   (1) *The Register of the Freeman of Norwich 1548-1713*, Norwich (1934)

            (2) *The Freeman of Norwich 1714-1752*, Norfolk Record Society, volume 23 (1952)

Newman F   *Two Centuries of Mancroft Music*, no place of publication (1932)

Overton J H   *The Nonjurors, their lives, principles and writings*, London (1902)

Peile J   *Biographical Register of Christ's College 1505-1905*, Cambridge (1910)

Roast T R   (1) *Composers of Norwich Cathedral 1620-1819*, unpublished dissertation for the degree of PhD, University of East Anglia (1998)

            (2) 'The Beckwiths of Norwich', *British Music*, volume 18 (1996), pp. 1-11

(3) *Hospital Charity Services at Norwich Cathedral 1773-1823*, Norwich (2002)

(4) *A Catalogue of the Old Music Manuscripts at Norwich Cathedral*, Norwich (2010)

Saunders H W   *A History of the Norwich Grammar School*, Norwich (1932)

Shaw H W   *The Succession of Organists: of the Chapel Royal and the Cathedrals of England and Wales from c. 1538*, Oxford (1991)

Sinclair J   *Sketches of Old Times and Distant Places*, London (1875)

Stephen G A   *The Waits of the City of Norwich through four Centuries to 1790*, Norfolk and Norwich Archaeological Society (1933)

Turner D   *List of Norfolk Benefices, with the names of their respective Incumbents and Patrons, and the Dates of the Several Presentations*, Norwich (1847)

Venn J and Venn J A   *Alumni Cantabrigienses, a biographical list of all known students, graduates and holders of office at the University of Cambridge from the earliest times to 1900*, part I to 1751, 4 volumes, Cambridge (1922)

Venn J A   *Alumni Cantabrigienses, ... to 1900*, part II from 1752-1900, 6 volumes, Cambridge (1940)

Williams J F and Cozens-Hardy B   *Extracts from the two earliest Minute Books of the Dean and Chapter of Norwich Cathedral, 1566-1649*, Norfolk Record Society, volume 24 (1953)

Wilson R G   'The Cathedral in the Georgian Period, 1720-1840', *Norwich Cathedral: Church, City and Diocese 1096-1996*, London (1996)